Fixed Income and Interest Rate Derivative Analysis

Fixed Income and Interest Rate Derivative Analysis

Mark Britten-Jones

OXFORD AMSTERDAM BOSTON LONDON NEW YORK PARIS
SAN DIEGO SAN FRANCISCO SINGAPORE SYDNEY TOKYO

Butterworth-Heinemann
An imprint of Elsevier Science
Linacre House, Jordan Hill, Oxford OX2 8DP
200 Wheeler Road, Burlington, MA 01803

First published 1998
Transferred to digital printing 2003

British Library Cataloguing in Publication Data
A catalogue record for this book is available from the British Library

Library of Congress Cataloguing in Publication Data
A catalogue record for this book is available from the Library of Congress

ISBN 0 7506 4012 X

For information on all Butterworth-Heinemann publications
visit our website at www.bh.com

Printed and bound in Great Britain by Antony Rowe Ltd, Eastbourne

Contents

Preface

Participants in today's fixed income markets need to know not only details of particular instruments such as Treasury bonds, corporate bonds, mortgages, swaps, etc. but also the analytical framework and techniques required for pricing and hedging. Although many good descriptions of particular instruments and market conventions are readily available, the explosive growth in analytical methods in recent years has meant that many analytical results are only available in journals or working papers. Many of these articles are written at a very high level of mathematical abstraction, resulting in many analytical tools being unavailable to the general reader.

The central thesis of this text is that the fundamentals of fixed income and interest rate derivative analysis are simple and can be easily understood not as high-powered mathematical formulas, but as a small number of simple economic concepts. From these simple principles a wide range of fixed income instruments and derivatives can be valued and hedged:

- Fixed cash flows can be valued using the principle of static replication. The underlying concept is no more difficult than the notion of pricing a basket of shopping goods given the prices of the individual goods.

- More complex cashflows such as FRAs, inverse floaters, futures, and simple swaps can be understood, valued, and hedged using the concept of simple dynamic replication.

- Generalized interest-rate-sensitive cash flows such as caps and floors, bond options, and callable bonds can also be valued and hedged using the concept of replication. However, replication now takes place within the context of a specific model, and the merits and drawbacks of various types of model are discussed.

The simplicity of the underlying economic principles provides a unifying theme to the text. In general, these concepts are reinforced and amplified not with high-powered mathematics, but with actual examples of various market instruments. In this manner a large number of instruments is covered without sacrificing the analysis essential to a true understanding of the instruments.

A second theme is the incorporation of real world frictions such as transactions costs and short-selling constraints into the analytical framework. Though often ignored, such considerations are vital when making choices in the market.

Acknowledgements

Very little in this book is original material. As such I am greatly indebted to the finance faculty at UCLA, especially Michael Brennan and Mark Grinblatt. I would also like to thank my colleagues at London Business School, especially Stephen Schaeffer, Anthony Neuberger, and Ian Cooper, for their invaluable insights. Lastly, I would like to thank the students in the Masters in Finance and the MBA programs at LBS, who have taken my Fixed Income course and provided much feedback on the material presented here.

Part I
Fixed Cash Flows

Fixed cash flows form the building blocks of all default-free bonds, and as such comprise a large proportion of the world bond market. Traditionally, fixed income analysis starts with the (quite complex) formula for determining the *yield-to-maturity* of a bond. The approach we use starts with zero-coupon bond prices.

The central thesis of this part is that any default-free bond with fixed cash flows can be viewed simply as a portfolio of zero-coupon bonds. This approach is not only easier than the traditional approach, it is also more useful. It is easy because determining any bond's value is simple (multiply and add) once we have the underlying zero prices. It is more useful because valuation and hedging are not separate concepts: valuation is done by forming a synthetic portfolio of zero-coupon bonds with known costs that replicates the original instrument. A short position in this synthetic portfolio must then hedge the value of the original instrument.

The first chapter explores these ideas in detail, and relates them to traditional measures of bond value such as yield-to-maturity. We also show how implied zero prices can be estimated when actual zero-coupon bonds are not traded in the market.

In practice, perfect replication of an arbitrary set of fixed cash flows is often not possible. In Chapter Two we show that, in this case, various techniques for approximate replication are useful for hedging purposes.

Chapter 1

Valuation of fixed cash flows with perfect replication

The bedrock fundamental concept in fixed income analysis, is that in a competitive market we can use the Law of One Price to value a security once we have calculated the security's cash flows and we have observed or calculated zero-coupon bond prices. The first half of the chapter explains the Law of One Price as it relates to fixed income. The second half of the chapter describes the cash flows and market conventions of standard US Treasury securities and shows how to calculate implied zero-coupon bond prices when zeros are not actually traded.

1.1 Implications of a competitive market

Much of fixed income is concerned with the valuation of payments that are promised for a future specified date. For example a straight Treasury bond promises to make payments with the amount and date of the payments determined by the face value, maturity date, and coupon rate of the bond (we shall see what exactly is promised by a US Treasury bond shortly). Because the cash flows are certain we are not worried about the risk of default or the volatility of the cash flow. Instead all information about the cash flow is summarized by two numbers (i) the amount; and (ii) the date of the cash flow.

To make things simple consider a single payment of one dollar that is promised for a known future date. The question we are interested in is — how much would a particular individual be willing to pay today for this promised payment in the future? The obvious answer perhaps, is that it would depend on the individual. Some individuals might be willing to pay more or less than others depending on their need for cash now, compared to their expected need for cash at the future date. The answer then may seem to be subjective and arbitrary depending on the individual. There can therefore be no 'universal' value assigned to a future payment of one dollar. It is a remarkable fact that this line of reasoning, under certain assumptions is incorrect. Under the assumption that a competitive market exists for the buying and selling of future payments, there exists a unique value (which is simply a price) for a dollar payable at the future date.

What's a competitive market? If individuals believe they can buy or sell as much as they want of a particular good at the market price, then the market in that good is called competitive. That's all. It is worth examining the immediate implications of a competitive market for future (i.e. promised) cash flows.

First, a competitive market requires that there be no transaction costs such as commission charges, brokerage fees, or bid–ask spreads. This follows simply from the fact that you can buy *or* sell at *one* price. Transaction costs introduce a wedge between buying and selling prices. This wedge is either explicit in the form of a bid–ask spread, or implicit after adding fees on to the purchase price or subtracting fees from the selling price.

Second, a competitive market assumes some unspecified but effective *enforcement* mechanism for promised payments. We have thus assumed away default risk.

The competitive market assumption is the logical place to start for the analysis of fixed income securities, and we shall see that it is adequate for many purposes. For other purposes however, the assumptions of zero default risk and zero transactions costs impede correct analysis and profitable decision-making. Accordingly we introduce in Part II transaction costs, or bid–ask spreads into the analysis. The risk of default is so important that we devote a whole chapter to it.

But for now, let's assume that a competitive market exists for the sale and purchase of future dollars. What does this imply?

1.1.1 The Law of One Price

A competitive market implies that there exists a single price today (date 0) for a dollar promised for a future date T. We call this price today $B(0, T)$, where the 0 tells us that the price is of today, and the T tells us that the one dollar will be paid at a date in T years time. Time is always measured in years in this book unless otherwise specified. There is a *single* price because only one price can exist for any commodity that is traded in a competitive market. Why? Well if a competitive market exists for a commodity, then if there are two different prices, you could buy as much as you wanted at the lower price, and sell as much as you wanted at the higher price (remember that in a competitive market you can buy or sell as much as you want at market prices). By doing this on a scale of your choosing you could make as much money as you chose. For this not to be possible there must be a single price for all commodities. This result is called, somewhat unimaginatively, the 'Law of One Price', and the argument we have just used to prove it is called a *no-arbitrage* argument or condition.

The strategy of buying low, selling high, and becoming as rich as we desire, is called an arbitrage strategy. By requiring that no-arbitrage strategies exist, we produce a restriction on possible prices (in this case, that any commodity can only have one price). We shall use many different forms of no-arbitrage conditions to price securities, but the above argument is perhaps the most fundamental.

The assumption of competitive markets for future cash flows results in a valuation formula for any fixed, i.e. non-random, payment at date T. Just as the price of three apples is three times the price of one apple, so a payment at date T of $C(T)$ dollars has value

$$\begin{pmatrix} \text{Value today of} \\ \text{payment of } C \\ \text{at date } T \end{pmatrix} = C(T) \times B(0,T)$$

This is a very simple linear relationship. Simply multiply the number of future dollars to be paid $C(T)$ by the price of a future dollar $B(0,T)$. The price of a future dollar $B(0,T)$ is also called the *discount factor*, reflecting the fact that the value of a future dollar must be discounted back to give the value today.

What about multiple dates at which payments will be made? A typical bond will make coupon payments at semi-annual or annual intervals, as well as a principal payment at maturity. How can we arrive at a single figure for the value of all these separate payments? The answer can be deduced from the 'Principle of Value Additivity'.

The 'Principle of Value Additivity' simply states that the value of a collection of commodities is equal to the sum of the value of each.

Alternatively, we can say that the value of the whole equals the sum of the value of the parts. If apples are selling at one dollar and bananas are selling for 50 cents then the value of an apple and banana together must equal $1.50. This principle results again from the no-arbitrage condition. If some portfolio was valued differently from the sum of its parts then it should be possible to make an infinite sum of money by either buying the parts and selling the portfolio or buying the portfolio and selling the parts.

The key to valuing payments at different future dates is to view dollars promised at different future dates as separate commodities. We then value each payment at each date using the discount factor (price) for that date and then simply sum the values across all the payment dates. Thus for a set of cash flows of amount $C(t_i)$ at dates $t_1, t_2, \ldots, t_N$ (i.e. cash flows to be received in $t_1, t_2, \ldots, t_N$ years time) the value is given by the following formula where the symbol $B(0, t_i)$ is the discount factor for a cash flow at date t_i:

$$\text{Value today} = \sum_{i=1}^{N} C(t_i) \times B(0, t_i)$$

The closest instrument in reality to a promised payment at a future date is a zero-coupon bond. For US Treasuries there is an active market for zeros that have been 'stripped' from the original bonds. The prices of these zeros provide an unusually accurate and easily obtainable measure of the discount factors $B(0, t_i)$ for the dates at which Treasury bonds make their payments.

Example 1 *The following table contains US Treasury strip prices for 25 October 1996.*

Date	Bid	Ask
Nov 97	*94:11*	*94:12*
Nov 98	*88:24*	*88:26*
Nov 99	*83:08*	*83:11*
Nov 00	*78:04*	*78:06*
Nov 01	*73:06*	*73:09*

What is the value as of 25 October 1996 for payments of $500 annually starting Nov 97 and stopping Nov 2001? First, note that US Treasury bonds are quoted in 1/32s assuming a face value of $100. Second, we shall ignore the bid–ask spread *and use the average of bid and ask prices. The value is then given as*

$$Value = 500 \left(\frac{94 + \frac{11.5}{32}}{100} \right) + 500 \left(\frac{88 + \frac{25}{32}}{100} \right) + 500 \left(\frac{83 + \frac{9.5}{32}}{100} \right)$$

$$+ 500 \left(\frac{78 + \frac{5}{32}}{100} \right) + 500 \left(\frac{73 + \frac{7.5}{32}}{100} \right)$$

$$= 471.797 + 443.906 + 416.484 + 390.781 + 366.172$$

$$= \$2089.14$$

Once a set of discount factors is obtained we can value all fixed cash flows very easily using the above approach. The simplicity of this approach which only involves multiplication and addition stems directly from the principle of value additivity.

1.1.2   Implied zero prices

If zero-coupon bonds need to be traded to use the Law of One Price then, it would have much less applicability than it in fact has. In most countries, zero-coupon bonds are not actively traded, but the Law of One Price can be used to derive a unique set of implied zero prices from the prices of actively traded fixed income securities. There are two techniques. The first, and simpler method is known as 'bootstrapping', and we examine it first. The second method known as 'inversion' is more powerful, and we recommend it when there are many bonds of differing maturities.

Bootstrapping

This method is best illustrated by an example. Say we have a 1 year note (FV = \$100) with price P_1, and a 2 year 10% coupon bond with price P_2. The one-year discount factor is given directly from the first bond:

$$B(0, 1) = P_1/100$$

The problem is to calculate the 2 year discount factor. The difficulty is that the 2 year bond has an intermediate payment, and we desire the price of a single cash flow occurring in 2 years time. To do this write the bond pricing formula for the 2 year bond:

$$P_2 = B(0,1)10 + B(0,2)110$$

and now strip the payment at one year away,

$$P_2 - B(0,1)10 = B(0,2)110$$

and solve for the 2 year discount factor:

$$B(0,2) = \frac{P_2 - B(0,1)10}{110}$$

The method is called bootstrapping because you move sequentially from short bonds to longer bonds, using the zero rates you have previously derived to strip out the intermediate coupons of the next maturity bond. This then gives you the next zero rate enabling you to strip out the last but one coupon payment of the *next* maturity bond, etc.

This method is obviously time-consuming to do, especially if you want zero rates at semi-annual intervals going out many years. The inversion method is easier once understood, though it does require matrix algebra.

Inversion method

In this method we fill in a matrix (table) in which each row contains the cash flows of *one* bond. Each entry represents the payment at a particular date. For a 1 year note, a 2 year 10% coupon bond, and a 3 year 6% bond the table would look as follows:

$$C = \begin{bmatrix} 100 & 0 & 0 \\ 10 & 110 & 0 \\ 6 & 6 & 106 \end{bmatrix}$$

We call this matrix C for cash flow matrix. Now we put the bond prices in a column vector:

$$P = \begin{bmatrix} P_1 \\ P_2 \\ P_3 \end{bmatrix}$$

where $P_1, \ldots, P_3$ are the prices of the bonds. Labelling the discount factors by $B(0,1), B(0,2)$, and $B(0,3)$ we have that:

$$\begin{bmatrix} P_1 \\ P_2 \\ P_3 \end{bmatrix} = \begin{bmatrix} 100B(0,1) + 0B(0,2) + 0B(0,3) \\ 10B(0,1) + 110B(0,2) + 0B(0,3) \\ 6B(0,1) + 6B(0,2) + 106B(0,3) \end{bmatrix}$$

In matrix notation we write this as

$$P = CB$$

$$P = \begin{bmatrix} 100 & 0 & 0 \\ 10 & 110 & 0 \\ 6 & 6 & 106 \end{bmatrix} \begin{bmatrix} B(0,1) \\ B(0,2) \\ B(0,3) \end{bmatrix}$$

This is an equation which we need to solve for the ds to give us the zero prices from which we can get the zero rates. To solve we use matrix inversion:

$$B = C^{-1}P$$

$$\begin{bmatrix} B(0,1) \\ B(0,2) \\ B(0,3) \end{bmatrix} = \begin{bmatrix} 100 & 0 & 0 \\ 10 & 110 & 0 \\ 6 & 6 & 106 \end{bmatrix}^{-1} \begin{bmatrix} P_1 \\ P_2 \\ P_3 \end{bmatrix}$$

This is easily done using a spreadsheet package such as Excel.[1] If you need to recalculate zero rates when prices change all you need to change are the prices, the cash flow matrix will remain the same until a coupon payment occurs.

Example 2 *Calculate discount factors for the next five semi-annual payment dates of US Treasury bonds using the following US Treasury bond information.*

Technical note

If there are more bonds than dates then you can calculate a 'best-fit' set of zero prices by using the 'regression' formula

$$B = (C'C)^{-1}C'P$$

where B is the required vector of zero-coupon prices, and C is now a rectangular matrix with the number of rows equalling the number of bonds, and

---

[1] In Excel to invert a matrix (array in Excel terminology) proceed as follows. First select a blank square area equal in size to the matrix you wish to invert. This area will contain the matrix inverse. Next type: = `minverse(A1:C3)`, where you will need to choose the appropriate cell references for the upper-left and lower-right corners of the original matrix. Next, press CTRL-Shift-Enter and you should have the inverted matrix.

the number of columns equalling the number of payment dates. In Excel you do not actually need to do this calculation. Instead simply regress bond prices onto cash flows. In regression terminology each column corresponding to a particular date is an explanatory variable and the regression coefficient associated with it is the implied discount factor.

1.2   Zero prices and market conventions

Unfortunately although a discount factor or zero price is simple and logical, the most common way of expressing the time-value of money is in terms of interest rates, and it is here that difficulties start. The reason is that interest rates can be calculated in many different ways, and indeed are calculated in many different ways in different markets. The relation between the various sorts of interest rates and the discount factor is shown below for the three major types of interest rates. We then examine the market conventions in the US Treasury markets.

1.2.1   Interest rates

The three forms of interest rate that are most commonly used are discount rates, simple interest rates, and compounded rates. Continuously compounded rates are often used for analytical purposes. It is important therefore to become familiar with these forms of interest rates. All formulas give rates in *decimal notation* meaning that a 7% rate for example is given from the formula as 0.07. To convert the rates to percentage rates simply multiply by 100.

Discount rates

Discount rates are used in the T-bill spot and futures markets. The discount rate $i_d(T)$ over the period T days[2] is defined by

$$B(0, T) = 1 - i_d(T)\frac{T}{360}$$

$$i_d(T) = \frac{360}{T}(1 - B(0, T))$$

---

[2] Note that here time T is measured in days, and we therefore need to divide by 360.

Example 3 *The 3 month (91 day) Treasury bill rate is 4.65%. What is the 91 day discount factor? Use the above formula to give:*

$$B(0, 91 \ days) = 1 - \frac{0.046\,5 \times 91}{360}$$

$$= 0.988\,25$$

Two things worth noting are the fact that 360 days are úsed, as this is the US market convention, and that the discount factor (bill price) is linear in the discount rate. We shall see that linearity of price and interest rate is the exception rather than the rule.

Simple interest rates

Interest rate derivatives, such as swaps, often use simple interest rates in contract specification. The simple interest rate $i_s(T)$ over the period T days is given by

$$B(0, T) = \frac{1}{1 + \left(i_s(T) \times \frac{T}{365}\right)}$$

$$i_s(T) = \left(\frac{1}{B(0, T)} - 1\right) \frac{365}{T}$$

This expression assumes no compounding. It is simply the growth rate scaled (i.e. divided) by the number of years, where this number may be a fraction. Note that the price–rate relation is not linear.

Discretely compounded rates

Annually compounded rates are used in the Eurodollar market. The formula for the annually compounded rate $i_c(T)$ over T years (where T may be a fraction #days/360) is

$$B(0, T) = \frac{1}{(1 + i_c(T))^T}$$

$$i_c(T) = \left(\frac{1}{B(0, T)}\right)^{\frac{1}{T}} - 1$$

Semi-annually compounded rates are used in the US Treasury market. The formula for a semi-annually compounded rate $i_{1/2}(T)$ for a period of T years is

$$B(0,T) = \frac{1}{\left(1 + \frac{i_c(T)}{2}\right)^{2T}}$$

$$i_c(T) = 2\left(\left(\frac{1}{B(0,T)}\right)^{\frac{1}{2T}} - 1\right)$$

Note that the actual payment of coupons is irrelevant for the calculation of these rates. All these examples have used zero-coupon bonds. Note also that all rates have been expressed as per annum rates. This is quite separate from the compounding frequency.

Continuous compounding

If we measure time t in years and compound n times per year at a rate r, then one dollar will grow to

$$\left(1 + \frac{r}{n}\right)^{nt}$$

in t years time. It can be shown that as we compound more and more frequently (i.e. as $n \to \infty$) one dollar will grow to

$$e^{rt} \equiv \exp(rt)$$

Recall that t is measured in years and that r must be expressed in decimal notation.

The number $e = 2.7183\ldots$ and its counterpart the natural logarithm $\ln$ is as important in sophisticated fixed income modelling as the number π is to a surveyor. Accordingly we need to know something about its properties. The following is meant as a handy reference. More detailed information is available from any mathematics text.

Eight rules of e

1. $\ln e^x = x$
2. $e^{\ln x} = x$
3. $\ln xy = \ln x + \ln y$

4. $\ln\left(\frac{x}{y}\right) = \ln x - \ln y$

5. $e^a \times e^b = e^{a+b}$

6. $(e^a)^T = e^{aT}$

7. $\frac{de^x}{dx} = e^x$

8. $\frac{d\ln x}{dx} = \frac{1}{x}$

Recall that the price of 1 dollar delivered in t years time is $B(0,t)$. This does not depend on methods of compounding, market conventions, etc. The continuously compounded spot rate $r_c(t)$ (the c subscript denotes continuous compounding) is defined by:

$$B(0,t)\exp(t \times r_c(t)) = 1$$

Now we can use some of the math we have learned to derive some rather elegant expressions.

$$\ln\left(B(0,t)\exp(t \times r_c(t))\right) = \ln 1$$

$$\ln B(0,t) + (t \times r_c(t)) = 0$$

Therefore the continuously compounded rate is simply minus the log of the zero price divided by the maturity:

$$r_c(t) = \frac{-\ln B(0,t)}{t}$$

1.2.2   US Treasury bonds and bills

The market in US Treasury securities is the second largest component of the world bond market (after the US mortgage market). As Treasury securities are backed by the US Government, the securities are widely viewed as being default-free. The Treasury issues two types of security: discount securities which only make a principal repayment at maturity and coupon securities which make coupon payments in addition to the principal payment.

US Treasury bonds and notes

Securities with maturities between two and ten years (when issued) are called Treasury notes. These make coupon payments every six months.

For example a Treasury note with a coupon of 10% and maturity date of August 2004 would make payments of $5 (per face value of $100) every February and August until August 2004 when a payment of $105 is made. Coupon and principal payments are made on the 15th day of the relevant month. Treasury Bonds have maturities of greater than ten years when issued, and, prior to 1985, some Treasury bonds were callable. The values of T-notes and T-bonds are normally expressed either in terms of a price or a yield.

Quoted prices and accrued interest   Prices are normally quoted as a percentage of face value, with a typical increment of $\frac{1}{32}$. Thus a price quote of 92:10 on a bond with $1 m face value translates into a price of $923\,125$:

$$923\,125 = \left(92 + \frac{10}{32}\right) \times 1\,000\,000$$

The price quoted in newspapers or on screens is the *quoted* or *clean* price. *It is not the price actually paid.* In addition to paying the quoted price on settlement day (the next business day), the buyer must in addition, pay to the seller that part of the next coupon payment that by convention he is deemed to deserve. Say there are 182 days from last coupon payment to the next, and that settlement occurs 60 days after the last coupon payment. Then the extra payment is calculated as

$$\frac{60}{182}\left(\frac{c}{2}\right)$$

This extra payment is called the *accrued interest*, and the actual price paid is called the *gross* or *full* price. The gross price is the true price or actual value of the security, so one must always adjust quoted prices for accrued interest.

$$\text{Gross price} = \text{Quoted price} + \text{AI}$$

where AI is given by

$$\text{AI} = \left(\frac{c}{2}\right)\left(\frac{t_{is}}{N_d}\right)$$

$$c \equiv \text{coupon rate},$$

$$t_{is} \equiv \text{days from last coupon to settlement, and}$$

$$N_d \equiv \text{number of days in current coupon period.}$$

Yield-to-maturity   Also given in newspapers is the yield-to-maturity (y-t-m) of a bond. This is the single rate which sets the present value of all cash flows to the gross price of the bond. The actual formula is

$$P_g = \frac{1}{1 + y/2)^{t_{sc}/N_d}} \left[\sum_{k=1}^{n} \frac{c/2}{(1 + y/2)^{k-1}} + \frac{1}{(1 + y/2)^{n-1}} \right]$$

where,

$$P_g \equiv \text{gross price,}$$
$$y \equiv \text{yield-to-maturity,}$$
$$t_{sc} \equiv \text{days from settlement to next coupon date,}$$
$$N_d \equiv \text{days in coupon period, and}$$
$$n \equiv \text{number of future coupons.}$$

Yield is a convenient way of expressing price — and nothing more. It is an inherently flawed concept as it applies the same discount rate to different cash flows, rather like talking about an average price of apples and oranges, without mentioning the relative quantities of apples and oranges. Bonds with the same maturity will have different yields if their coupons differ and if the yield curve is not flat. If one bond yields more than another it does not mean that it is better value. You need to look at the cash flows that underlie the bond.

US Treasury bills

US Treasury bills pay no coupons and are issued with maturities of 3, 6, and 12 months. Price is conventionally quoted as an annualized percentage discount from face value. Thus a typical quote might be 6%. To calculate the price of the bill insert the discount in the following formula:

$$\text{T-bill price} = \text{face value} \times \left[1 - \left(\frac{\% \text{ discount}}{100} \times \frac{\text{days to maturity}}{360} \right) \right]$$

Note that the discount is not a rate of return, because it is calculated as a percentage of the final value of the bill, not the initial investment. An accepted practice has developed which gives a T-bill's *bond equivalent yield*.

For bonds maturing in less than six months the formula is

$$y = \frac{100 - P}{P} \times \frac{365}{\text{days to maturity}}$$

This figure is simply the annualized return. Note that the price of the T-bill is *linear* in the discount, i.e. there is no convexity of price in terms of the discount.

1.2.3   What is a par bond?

A par bond is a (coupon-paying) bond which is selling at face value. Some investment banks produce a par yield curve. This is a hypothetical construct in which a bond is constructed with a coupon rate such that it sells at par. The par yield curve is then simply a plot of these coupon rates against maturity. A plot of actual y-t-ms of various bonds against the maturities of bonds, is a rather senseless device. The y-t-m will depend on coupon payments as well as maturity, but the y-t-m graph does not show the level of coupon. The par yield curve provides information on both the coupon and the y-t-m, and for this reason is a better analytical device. Given a set of discount factors we can construct a par yield curve by simply solving for the coupon that sets the bond's price to par. For a bond with N annual coupon payments we have:

$$100 = \sum_{i=1}^{N} C \times B(0, t_i) + 100 B(0, t_N)$$

$$C_N(\%) = \frac{100(1 - B(0, t_N))}{\sum_{i=1}^{N} B(0, t_i)}$$

Par bonds and par yields have some interesting arithmetical properties. In particular they allow extremely simple 'bootstrapping' for calculation of discount factors, if we are ever presented with a par yield curve and need to know implied zero prices. Understanding the following trick will enhance your understanding of basic bond math. Say we have calculated the discount factor $B(0, t_{N-1})$ and know the par yields C_N and C_{N-1}, and we want to calculate the next discount factor $B(0, t_N)$. Proceed as follows: first separate

$B(0, t_N)$ from the summation:

$$C_N(\%) = \frac{100(1 - B(0, t_N))}{B(0, t_N) + \sum\limits_{i=1}^{N-1} B(0, t_i)}$$

Rearranging this expression gives

$$B(0, t_N) = \frac{100 - C_N \sum\limits_{i=1}^{N-1} B(0, t_i)}{100 + C_N} \qquad (1.1)$$

We do not know the term $\sum_{i=1}^{N-1} B(0, t_i)$, but this is easily calculated from the expression for C_{N-1}:

$$C_{N-1} = \frac{100(1 - B(0, t_{N-1}))}{\sum\limits_{i=1}^{N-1} B(0, t_i)}$$

$$\sum_{i=1}^{N-1} B(0, t_i) = \frac{100(1 - B(0, t_{N-1}))}{C_{N-1}}$$

Insert this expression back into (1.1) and we are done:

$$B(0, t_N) = \frac{100 - C_N \left(\frac{100(1 - B(0, t_{N-1}))}{C_{N-1}} \right)}{100 + C_N}$$

1.3   Fitting the treasury strip curve

The methods outlined in Section 1.1.2 give a set of discount factors at particular (discrete dates). To value cash flows occurring at other dates, some form of interpolation is commonly used. The following is based on a simplification of the procedure in 'Semi-Empirical Smooth Fit to the Treasury Yield Curve' by Paul Diament in *The Journal of Fixed Income* June 1993. Take as our starting point a set of prices for 'Treasury strips'. This provides a set of discount factors at specific dates (quarterly for the closer maturities).

We want to find a continuous curve that fits the data well, is differentiable (for easy calculation of forward prices), and does not necessarily pass through every point as this may result in 'errors' due to stale prices or liquidity differences producing bizarre implied forward rate behaviour. The procedure we outline requires nonlinear optimization a formerly esoteric tool now widely available to all via the Excel Solver command (in the Tools menu). The procedure is as follows:

1. Convert zero prices to continuously compounded spot rates using the *In* function and the *days 360* function to calculate exact fractional years for calculation of maturity.

2. Use four cells to contain the parameter values of R, r, T_0 and a. Select starting values using interpretations given in the paper.

3. For each maturity t calculate a predicted yield using the following formula:
$$\frac{R \cdot (t/T_0)^a + r}{(t/T_0)^a + 1}$$

4. For each maturity calculate the error or difference between actual and predicted yields, and then square the error.

5. Sum the errors and place the result in a specific cell.

6. Choose Solver from the Tools menu, select Minimization of the cell containing the sum of squared errors, and select the four cells containing the input parameters as the cells which Solver is allowed to change. Press OK.

Solver should now find the values of R, r, T_0, and a which provide the best fit. If this fit is unsatisfactory you should try the alternative formula contained in the paper on p. 68. Note that this requires an extra parameter. An instantaneous forward rate curve can now be estimated as follows.

$$f_t = \frac{d \ln(P(t))}{dt} = \frac{dR^c(t) \cdot t}{dt}$$

Using the product rule this gives:

$$f_t = R_t^c + t \cdot \frac{dR_t^c}{dt} = R_t^c + t \cdot \frac{(R - R^c(t)) \cdot (R^c(t) - r)}{(R - r) \cdot t}$$

and this can be calculated from the parameters given by Solver. The result is that you should now have good estimates of a continuous spot rate curve and of a continuous instantaneous forward rate curve.

1.4   Further reading

1. Carleton, W.T. and I. Cooper (1982) 'Estimation and Uses of the Term Structure of Interest Rates' *Journal of Finance* 31(4), p. 1067–1083.

2. Ronn, E.I. (1987) 'A New Linear Programming Approach to Bond Portfolio Management' *Journal of Financial and Quantitative Analysis* 22(4), p. 439–466.

1.5   Questions

1. Compare the price of a 5 year Treasury note with the price implied by valuing the T-note's cash flows using US Treasury strip prices. The *Wall Street Journal* has the necessary pricing information.

2. Use the Diament procedure to fit a smooth yield curve to US Treasury strip prices (obtainable from the *Wall Street Journal*).

Chapter 2

Imperfect replication: immunization and duration

Consider an insurance firm whose liabilities involve payments that the company can predict quite accurately. The firm needs to invest the premiums it receives today into a portfolio of assets, so that it can be sure of meeting the payments, and it wants to do so at as low a cost as possible.

Viewing the future payments as fixed, the ideal strategy would simply invest the premiums in default-free bonds, with the bonds selected so that bond cash flows exactly offset the future payments.

For example, say an insurance firm has accurately estimated liabilities of $100 in 4 years time and $200 in 5 years time. By purchasing one 4 year zero-coupon bond with face value of $100 and two 5 year zeros with face values of $100 the insurance firm can be sure of meeting its obligations. The cost of this portfolio is given by the usual formula

$$100 \times B(0,4) + 200 \times B(0,5)$$

and it should be obvious that this is the cheapest (lowest cost) portfolio that is guaranteed to meet the liabilities. This approach is called (for obvious reasons) *cash flow matching*, but there is an alternative way of looking at the problem — in terms of *value tracking*.

If the portfolio of assets can be structured so that the value of the portfolio is always equal to the value of liabilities, then the liabilities can be met when they come due. For example, in the above case, the value of the liabilities at some future time t will be $100B(t,4) + 200B(t,5)$ where $B(t,4)$ and $B(t,5)$ are the prices at a future time t of dollars promised for year 4 and year 5 respectively. Clearly the value of the portfolio at time t is also given by

$100B(t,4) + 200B(t,5)$ and the portfolio value will perfectly track the value of liabilities. This shows the equivalence between cash flow matching and value tracking.

Often however cash flow matching is impossible. Liabilities may fall between coupon payment dates, or there may not be a full set of zero-coupon bonds. In this case, there will be an inevitable mismatch between the cash flows of the portfolio and the cash flows associated with the firm's liabilities.

The strategy in which a portfolio is constructed whose value will remain close to the value of liabilities, even though exact cash flow matching is not possible, is called *immunization* and this is the subject of this chapter. In general the goal of immunization is to construct a portfolio from some specified set of securities, such that the portfolio value will closely track the value of a *target portfolio*. In the above example the target portfolio was simply the estimated liabilities of the life insurance company.

The two simplest and most common methods of immunization are duration-matching and key rate analysis (also called 'bucket' analysis). We show how both methods can be easily implemented using spreadsheets and without using statistical analysis. More sophisticated techniques involving statistical analysis are examined in Chapter 4. We show that the key rate approach, though slightly more complex than the duration-matching approach, results in better immunization of the target portfolio.

2.1   Duration-matching

For centuries it has been known that bonds with longer maturities are riskier than bonds with shorter maturities. Moreover, it was also known that for bonds of a given maturity low coupon bonds were riskier than bonds with high coupons. In 1938 Frederic Macaulay published a paper in which he sought to characterize the riskiness of a bond by referring to both the maturity and coupon level of the bond. The concept he came up with is now called Macaulay duration and it forms the basis for the duration-matching approach to immunization.

2.1.1   Macaulay duration

The Macaulay duration of a bond is defined as the average weighted time to the payment of cash flows, where the weights are given by the fraction of total value accounted for by a particular cash flow. Assuming we are currently at a coupon date and that coupons are paid annually the formula for Macaulay duration is

$$D_{\text{Mac}} = \frac{\text{PV}(C_1) \cdot 1 + \text{PV}(C_2) \cdot 2 + \cdots + \text{PV}(C_T) \cdot T}{V_0}$$

where $\text{PV}(C_t) = C_t/(1+y)^t$ is the present value of cash flow C_t and $V_0 = \text{PV}(C_1) + \text{PV}(C_2) + \cdots + \text{PV}(C_T)$ is the present value of the cash flows. Note that we are using yield y to discount the cash flows and as argued before this is imprecise as the correct discounting rate should be a spot rate which will generally vary across dates. Another way to write this formula is as

$$D_{\text{Mac}} = \sum_{t=1}^{T} W_t \times t$$

where $W_t = \text{PV}(C_t)/V_0$ is a weight given by the proportion of the bond's value coming from the time t cash flow C_t. Note that these weights sum to one $\sum_{t=1}^{T} W_t = 1$ so that the weights can be thought of as fractions of total value.

Example 4 *Calculating Macaulay duration*

| *Coupon* | $7\frac{1}{4}\%$ | | *Maturity* | *29 Jan 05* |
| *yield* | 6.70% | | *settlement* | *6 May 1996* |
i	T_i	CF_i	$CF_i/(1+y)^{T_i}$	$T_i \times \dfrac{CF_i}{(1+y)^{T_i}}$
1	0.731	7.25	6.9143	5.0544
2	1.731	7.25	6.4802	11.217
3	2.731	7.25	6.0732	16.586
4	3.731	7.25	5.6919	21.236
5	4.731	7.25	5.3345	25.238
6	5.731	7.25	4.9995	28.652
7	6.731	7.25	4.6856	31.539
8	7.731	7.25	4.3914	33.95
9	8.731	107.25	60.883	531.57
Total			105.45	705.04
Macaulay duration			705.04/105.45	**= 6.686**

Bonds and Macaulay duration

Inspection of the above formula reveals several properties of duration. First, the duration of a zero-coupon bond or of a single cash flow C_t is simply the time to that cash flow t. Second, we can see that all bonds with coupon payments must have duration strictly less than maturity, and the higher the coupon rate the lower the duration other things being equal.

Portfolios and Macaulay duration

Duration is particularly simple to calculate for bond portfolios. For most purposes we can think of portfolio duration as simply the weighted average of the individual bond durations, where the weights are given by the fraction of portfolio value (PV) accounted for by each bond. Obviously the formula is almost identical to that used for calculating the duration of a particular bond, which of course we may think of as a portfolio of zero-coupon bonds. Can you see that this is not exactly correct? The reason being that a portfolio's duration should be calculated using the portfolio's yield to calculate the PVs of all the individual bonds. In practice this fact is ignored as it makes little difference, but it does illustrate the difficulties that arise when using the concept of yield.

2.1.2   Modified duration

The usefulness of Macaulay duration stems from the fact that it provides a guide to the riskiness of a bond. In fact a modified form of Macaulay's duration measure called, surprisingly enough, *modified duration* provides an exact (for small yield changes) expression for the percentage change in bond value resulting from a change in yield. And the sensitivity of bond price to changes in yield is commonly taken to be a measure of the riskiness of a bond. Again, this is not exactly correct because different bonds may have different yield volatilities. In fact longer bonds tend to exhibit less volatility in yields than short-term bonds, thus offsetting to some extent the riskiness of longer-term bonds resulting from greater yield sensitivity.

The formula for modified duration is as follows

$$D_{\text{mod}} = \frac{D_{\text{Mac}}}{1 + \frac{\text{yield}}{k}}$$

where k is the number of compounding periods per year (normally 1 or 2) used in the calculation of yield. Note that if we are using continuously compounded rates the Macaulay and modified durations are equivalent.

That modified duration does in fact describe the yield sensitivity is most easily seen by examining the price sensitivity of a zero-coupon bond. This is done by differentiating the zero-coupon bond price with respect to yield:

$$B(0, T) = \left(1 + \frac{y}{k}\right)^{-kT}$$

$$\frac{dB(0, T)}{dy} = -T\left(1 + \frac{y}{k}\right)^{-kT-1}$$

and then dividing both sides by price $B(0, T)$:

$$\frac{1}{B(0, T)} \frac{dB(0, T)}{dy} = \frac{-T}{1 + y/k} = -\frac{D_{\text{Mac}}}{1 + y/k}$$

$$= -D_{\text{mod}}$$

Many people have difficulties with the units of this equation. Duration will typically be a number between zero and thirty. A 10 year bond may have a duration of around 7 for example. This means that an increase in yield of 1 percentage point (100 basis points) results in the bond losing 7% of its value.

It is important to note that modified duration gives a percentage change in value not an absolute change in value. To calculate the change in value resulting from a yield change one needs to use modified duration and the actual value of the bond.

2.1.3   Duration-matching

The duration-matching approach to immunization, involves constructing a portfolio whose duration matches the duration of the target liability. The idea is that by so doing assets and liabilities will be equally sensitive to rate changes so that the discrepancy in value between assets and liabilities is minimized even though the cash flows are not perfectly matched. We first show how to do it. We then examine how well it works.

How to do it

The construction of a duration-matched immunization portfolio involves calculation of the duration of the target portfolio and calculation of the duration of the available hedging securities (the securities from which the immunizing portfolio will be constructed). Weights are then chosen so as to equate the duration of the hedge portfolio with the target portfolio. An example will make this clearer.

Example 5 *Suppose the target portfolio consists of payments of $100 for each of the next 4 years. We have two bonds from which we can construct an immunizing portfolio: a 1 year note and a 3 year bond with a 10% annual coupon. The current interest rate is 10%. The following table shows the relevant workings.*

TARGET PORTFOLIO

Time	Cash flow	Spot Rate	PV	PV × Time
1	100	10%	90.91	90.91
2	100	10%	82.64	165.28
3	100	10%	75.13	225.39
4	100	10%	68.30	273.20
Total			316.98	754.78

Duration (yrs) $2.381 = 754.78/316.98$
Mod. duration $\mathbf{2.16} = 2.381/1.10$

IMMUNIZING PORTFOLIO

1 year note

Time	Cash flow	Spot	PV	PV × Time
1	100	10%	90.91	90.91

Duration (yrs)   1
Mod. duration $\mathbf{0.909} = 1/1.10$

3 year 10%-coupon bond

Time	Cash flow	Spot	PV	PV × Time
1	10	10%	9.09	9.09
2	10	10%	8.26	16.52
3	110	10%	82.64	247.92
Total			100	273.53

Duration (yrs) $2.73 = 273.53/100$
Mod. duration $\mathbf{2.48} = 2.73/1.1$

Thus the liability stream has a modified duration of 2.16, the 1 year note has modified duration of 0.909 and the 3 year bond has modified duration of 2.48.

An immunizing portfolio must have value equal to the value of the target portfolio and duration equal to the duration of the target portfolio. We thus need to find weights W_1 and W_2 that satisfy

$$W_1 + W_2 = 1$$
$$W_1 \times 0.909 + W_2 \times 2.48 = 2.16$$

This is easily solved giving $W_1 = 0.203$, and $W_2 = 0.797$

An immunization portfolio by matching the duration of liabilities matches the rate sensitivity of liabilities so that both assets and liabilities will be equally affected by rate changes. So what can go wrong? Unfortunately, quite a lot can go wrong, as we shall see in the next section.

How well does duration-matching work?

You may have noticed a flaw in the logic of the duration-matching approach. Duration is based on yield and a yield is specific to a particular bond. Duration-matching results in the target and hedge portfolios having identical sensitivities to yield moves, but these yields are by definition not the same, being specific to each portfolio. There is no guarantee that the two yields will change in lockstep and this is what the duration-matching method implicitly assumes. In fact this overstates the case against duration. We show below that duration works quite well when *the spot rate curve shifts in a parallel fashion*. But when the spot curve tilts or flexes, a duration-matched hedge need not track the value of the target portfolio.

This point is very important and we shall illustrate it both algebraically and with a numerical example.

Duration and parallel yield curve moves

Consider the formula for valuing fixed cash flows $C(t_i)$ using continuously compounded spot rates $r(t_i)$:

$$V = \sum_{i=1}^{N} e^{(-t_i \cdot r(t_i))} C(t_i)$$

Now the spot rates $r(t_i)$ will, in general, all be different, but as we want to examine the effect of a parallel shift (i.e. all spot rates changing by the same

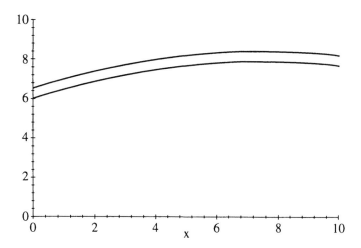

Figure 2.1 Parallel shift in the spot rate curve

amount) it will be useful to express the spot rate curve as a function of time. The following parameterization has the advantage of simplicity:

$$r(t_t) = a + b \cdot t_i + c \cdot t_i^2$$

Thus a is the intercept term, b controls the slope of the spot rate curve, and c controls the curvature of the spot rate curve. By varying a we can simulate parallel shifts in the curve. For example Figure 2.1 shows two spot rate curves where for the lower curve $a = 6.0$, $b = 0.5$, $c = -1/30$ and for the upper curve $a = 6.5$, $b = 0.5$, and $c = -1/30$.

The valuation formula can be written in terms of the spot curve parameterization

$$V = \sum_{i=1}^{N} \exp(-(a + b \cdot t_i + c \cdot t_i^2) \times t_i) \times C(t_i)$$

We can analyse the effect of a small parallel shift in the curve by differentiating the formula with respect to a:

$$\frac{dV}{da} = \sum_{i=1}^{N} -t_i \exp(-(a + b \cdot t_i + c \cdot t_i^2) \times t_i) \times C(t_i)$$

$$\frac{1}{V}\frac{dV}{da} = \sum_{i=1}^{N} \frac{-t_i \times \mathrm{PV}(t_i)}{V}$$

But this is simply the Macaulay duration of the bond (where the present values have been constructed 'correctly' using spot rates rather than a yield). This means that if a hedge portfolio is duration-matched to a target portfolio and the spot curve moves up or down in a parallel fashion then the value of the hedge portfolio will closely track the value of the target portfolio.

In the following example we show that when the yield curve does not move in parallel, the duration-matching approach does not work so well.

Example 6 *The target portfolio consists of a single cash flow of $100 in 10 years time. The current spot rate curve is flat at the 5% level, and the instruments available for the hedging portfolio are a 5 year zero-coupon bond and a 20 year zero. The hedge portfolio, constructed so as to have equal value and duration to the target portfolio, consists of 0.5225 of the 5 year zero and 0.5425 of the 20 year zero.*

Time (yrs)	PV	5	10	20	Duration
Spot rates		5%	5%	5%	
Target	61.39		100		9.52
Hedge	61.39	52.25		54.25	9.52

Parallel shift + 10 bp

		5	10	20	
Spot rates		5.1%	5.1%	5.1%	
Target	**60.81**		100		
Hedge	**60.81**	52.25		54.25	

Tilt

		5	10	20	
Spot rates		4.9%	5%	5.1%	
Target	**61.39**		100		
Hedge	**61.20**	52.25		54.25	

As can be seen when rates move in parallel the value of the hedge portfolio tracks the value of the target. However when the spot curve tilts upwards the hedge portfolio loses value by $0.19 whereas the target portfolio's value remains unchanged.

2.2   Key rate analysis

We have seen that duration-matching works well when the spot curve moves in a parallel fashion. In general empirical studies have found that although parallel type shifts are common, other types of spot curve move also frequently occur. In particular the spot curve can tilt so that the spot curve becomes steeper or flatter. Somewhat less frequently the spot curve flexes — meaning that the degree of curvature in the curve changes. In order to best immunize a target portfolio, under the assumption that a variety of spot curve moves are possible, a multifactor immunization technique called key rate analysis has been developed.

Key rates are particular rates selected by the analyst that are thought to adequately characterize the whole yield curve. By constructing a hedge portfolio that has the same sensitivities to each of the key rates, it is hoped that the value of the hedge portfolio will closely match the value of the target portfolio under general spot curve moves. Using key rate analysis for immunization involves four steps:

- selection of the key rates or spot curve 'drivers';
- specification of how other rates change in response to key rate changes;
- calculation of the sensitivities of the target portfolio to each of the key rates; and
- construction of a hedge portfolio which has the same sensitivities to each of the key rates as the target portfolio has.

We now illustrate these four steps.

2.2.1   Selection of key rates

The first step in construction of a key rate immunizing strategy is to select the key rates. The key rates will be the drivers or 'factors' of the model so their selection is important and several criteria need to be considered.

First the instruments underlying key rates should be liquid and actively traded so that the key rates will contain the latest information.

Second the key rates should be spread out across differing maturities so that the whole spot curve can be characterized. Finally a trade-off between hedging accuracy (with more key rates) and simplicity (fewer key rates) needs to be made. This will be determined in part by the nature of the target portfolio. For illustrative purposes we shall use key rates of 1 year, 3 years, 10 years, and 20 years. All rates are spot rates (i.e. for zero-coupon bonds).

2.2.2   Determination of other rates

We need to specify how all other spot rates change in response to changes in the key spot rates. This is done by assuming that the effect of a key rate change on other rates declines linearly with the distance (measured in time to maturity) from the key rate, reaching zero at adjacent key rates. The exception to this rule is for rates shorter than the first key rate. These are assumed to move one-to-one with the first key rate. Thus for the key rates selected above we have the following sensitivities:

1. Rates between 0 and 1 year: move directly with the 1 year rate, e.g. if 1 year rate increases by 10 basis points then 3 month and 6 month rates are assumed to also increase by 10 basis points.
2. Rates between 1 and 3 years: have sensitivities to both the 1 and the 3 year rate. The closer a rate's maturity is to 1 then the greater its sensitivity to the 1 year rate and the less its sensitivity to the 3 year rate. The 2 year rate will have sensitivity of 0.5 to both the 1 year and 3 year key rates. Sensitivity to other key rates is zero.
3. Rates between 3 and 10 years: have sensitivities to both the 3 and the 10 year rate. The closer a rate's maturity is to 3 then the greater its sensitivity to the 3 year rate and the less its sensitivity to the 10 year rate. Sensitivity to other key rates is zero. The same analysis applies for rates between 10 and 20 years.

This may sound complex but is in fact quite simple. Figures 2.2, 2.3 and 2.4 show how the spot curve moves in response to moves in each of the three key rates.

2.2.3   Calculation of target portfolio key rate durations

Although Macaulay duration is defined in terms of the timing of cash flows, it is also closely related to the sensitivity of the bond's value to changes in yield. We now define *key rate durations* as the sensitivity of bond value to a change in a key rate. The actual formula is

$$i\text{th key rate duration} \equiv -\frac{1}{P}\frac{dP}{dr_i}$$

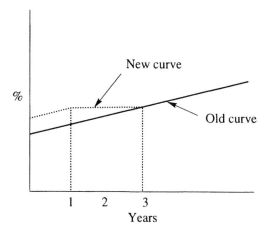

Figure 2.2 Spot rate curve: move in 1 year key rate

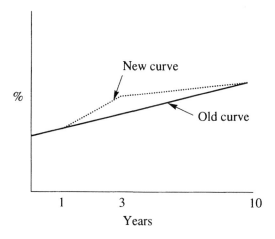

Figure 2.3 Spot rate curve: move in 3 year key rate

where r_i is the ith key rate and P is the value of the bond or portfolio. Instead of using derivatives we shall normally perturb each key rate by a small amount (say 10 bp) and then calculate the new price. Using this approach the formula is given by

$$i\text{th key rate duration} \equiv \frac{-1}{\text{Old price}} \times \frac{(\text{New price} - \text{Old price})}{(\text{New key rate} - \text{Old key rate})}$$

Again, an example will make this clearer.

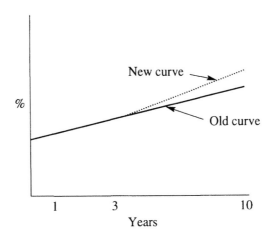

Figure 2.4 Spot rate curve: move in 10 year key rate

Example 7 *Imagine we have liabilities consisting of a 10% coupon (annual) 10 year bond. We revalue the bond under 10 basis point moves in each of the first three key rates as follows.*

			Key rate changes		
			1 yr *+10 bp*	*3 yr* *+10 bp*	*10 yr* *+10 bp*
Time	*Cash* *flows*	*Original* *spot rates*		*New spot rates*	
1	10	5.0	5.1	5.0	5.0
2	10	5.2	5.25	5.25	5.2
3	10	5.4	5.4	5.5	5.4
4	10	5.5	5.5	5.59	5.51
5	10	5.6	5.6	5.67	5.63
6	10	5.6	5.6	5.66	5.64
7	10	5.6	5.6	5.64	5.66
8	10	5.6	5.6	5.63	5.67
9	10	5.6	5.6	5.61	5.69
10	110	5.6	5.6	5.6	5.7
PV$		133.209	133.191	133.060	132.470
Key rate duration			**0.13**	**1.12**	**5.41**

The third column shows the original spot rate curve and the original value of the cash flows ($133.209). The next column shows the new spot curve following a 10 basis point increase in the 1 year rate. At the bottom of this column we show the present value of the cash flows under this altered spot rate curve. In the bottom row we have shown the key rate durations which are calculated in the following way using the 3 year key rate as an example:

$$3 \text{ yr duration} = \frac{-1}{133.209} \times \frac{(133.060 - 133.209)}{(0.055 - 0.054)}$$

$$= 1.12$$

2.2.4   Construction of a hedge portfolio

We must first specify the instruments that are available for construction of a hedge portfolio. For illustrative purposes we assume we can invest in overnight cash; a 1 year note; a 3 year 10% coupon bond, and a 6 year zero.

We then calculate the key rate durations of each of the hedging instruments. The calculated durations are shown in the following table. The method of calculation is identical to that used above for the target portfolio.

	Key rate durations		
	1 Year	3 Year	10 Year
Cash	0	0	0
1 yr note	0.952	0	0
3 yr 10%-coupon bond	0.157	2.449	0
6 yr zero	0	3.241	2.432

In order to construct a hedge portfolio we need to find weights that, first sum to one, and second result in a hedge portfolio with key rate durations equal to the key rate durations of the hedge portfolio. Now the key rate duration of a portfolio is easily calculated because a key rate duration like Macaulay duration is easily combinable across a portfolio. The portfolio key rate duration is simply the value-weighted average of the key rate durations of the bonds in the portfolio. We thus define a set of portfolio weights W_1, W_2, W_3, and W_4 that represent the fraction of portfolio value accounted for by each of the instruments. Note that all valuation is done using current market values. These conditions form a system of linear equations:

$$W_1 + W_2 + W_3 + W_4 = 1$$

and

$$0 \cdot W_1 + 0.952 \cdot W_2 + 0.157 \cdot W_3 + 0 \cdot W_4 = 0.13$$

$$0 \cdot W_1 + 0 \cdot W_2 + 2.449 \cdot W_3 + 3.241 \cdot W_4 = 1.12$$

$$0 \cdot W_1 + 0 \cdot W_2 + 0 \cdot W_3 + 2.432 \cdot W_4 = 5.41$$

This system of equations can easily be solved using matrix algebra:

$$
\begin{bmatrix}
1 & 1 & 1 & 1 \\
0 & 0.952 & 0.157 & 0 \\
0 & 0 & 2.449 & 3.241 \\
0 & 0 & 0 & 2.432
\end{bmatrix}
\begin{bmatrix}
W_1 \\ W_2 \\ W_3 \\ W_4
\end{bmatrix}
=
\begin{bmatrix}
1 \\ 0.13 \\ 1.12 \\ 5.41
\end{bmatrix}
$$

$$
\begin{bmatrix}
W_1 \\ W_2 \\ W_3 \\ W_4
\end{bmatrix}
=
\begin{bmatrix}
1 & 1 & 1 & 1 \\
0 & 0.952 & 0.157 & 0 \\
0 & 0 & 2.449 & 3.241 \\
0 & 0 & 0 & 2.432
\end{bmatrix}^{-1}
\times
\begin{bmatrix}
1 \\ 0.13 \\ 1.12 \\ 5.41
\end{bmatrix}
$$

$$
=
\begin{bmatrix}
0.71544 \\
0.54663 \\
-2.4866 \\
2.2245
\end{bmatrix}
$$

Thus the hedge portfolio involves depositing some cash at an overnight rate, investing an amount in the 1 year note, shorting a large amount of the 3 year coupon bond, and investing a large amount in the 6 year zero.

This completes our analysis of fixed cash flows. In Chapter 1 we saw that when we could exactly replicate the cash flows of a security using traded securities, then we could easily value and hedge the original security. In this Chapter we examined two techniques — duration-matching and key rate analysis — that could be used to construct hedging portfolios when exact replication was not possible. Working through the following assignment will help reinforce these ideas, as well as introduce you to an extremely useful tool in fixed income analysis — linear programming.

2.3 Further reading

Litterman, R. and J. Sheinkman (1991) 'Common Factors Affecting Bond Returns' *Journal of Fixed Income*, June, p. 54–61.

2.4 Questions

Pension fund X operates in the US Treasury Market. It accepts no new contributions, and is obligated to pay pensions to existing members. An actuary estimated liabilities stretching out 40 years. Valuing the liabilities using US T-bond rates the fund was in surplus. It was decided that about 60% of the fund should be invested in US Treasury bonds and the remainder invested in a US equity tracker fund. The bond component represented the present value of liabilities extending 10 years. The idea was to guarantee solvency for the next 10 years. The equity portion was designed to provide for longer liabilities and to hopefully allow pension increases above the minimum required.

The actual pattern of estimated liabilities was quite complex, but for illustrative purposes, we shall assume that liabilities consist of constant semi-annual payments of $US10 million. The value of these liabilities was set by the fund trustees as the performance benchmark for the fixed income part of the fund. The trustees stressed that benchmark tracking error must be very low. Duration bets were thus ruled out.

Your goal is to construct an immunization strategy that tracks the benchmark closely, and that benefits from any pricing anomalies that may arise in the market.

Asset universe consists of 2, 3, 5, 7, and 10 year coupon bonds (select one of each).

The Methodology that you will use has three steps:

1. calculation of a spot rate curve using linear programming;
2. calculation of key rate PVBPs for liabilities and for each bond in the asset universe; and
3. construction of a minimum cost portfolio that satisfies solvency conditions and matches key rate PVBPs.

2.4.1   Conservative spot curve construction

In the following we construct a spot curve that is conservative in the sense that it values liabilities as high as possible, consistent with the prices of bonds in the asset universe.

The linear programming (LP) problem is:

$$\max_{\{B(0,t_i)\}_{i=1}^n} 10m \sum_{i=1}^{n/2} B(0, t_{2i})$$

subject to

$$1 \geq B(0, t_1) \geq B(0, t_2) \geq \ldots \geq B(0, t_n) \text{ and}$$

$$P_j \geq \sum C_{t_i}^j B(0, t_i), \text{ for all bonds } j \text{ in the asset universe}$$

where $B(0, t_i)$ is the discount factor for date t_i; P_j is the price of bond j; and $C_{t_i}^j$ is the cash flow of bond j at date t_i.

The objective is simply the value of liabilities. The control variables are the set of discount factors. The first constraint is that the discount function be decreasing and less than 1. The second constraint is that we do not over-value the assets we can invest in.

This type of problem can be easily handled using the Solver function in Excel.

2.4.2   Calculation of PVBPs

PVBP (price value per basis point) of an instrument is simply the change in the instrument's value associated with a change in the reference yield of 1 basis point (0.01%). This can be calculated for a bond, but unlike duration, it can also be calculated for a zero-value position such as a swap, or a futures position.

The way to calculate PVBPs is to shock the spot curve, as outlined in Chapter 2, and then revalue each bond in the asset universe, and revalue the value of liabilities. The dollar change in value is the PVBP.

2.4.3   Minimum cost immunizing portfolio

We now need to construct a portfolio consisting of a set of holdings q_j of each bond in the asset universe. We select the set of weights in order to minimize cost subject to the value of assets being greater than liabilities, and the PVBPs of assets matching the PVBP of liabilities for each key rate.

Again we set this up as a linear programming problem:

$$\min_{\{q_j\}} \sum_j q_j P_j, \text{ subject to}$$

$$\sum_j q_j P_j \geq 10m \sum_{i=1}^{n/2} B(0, t_{2i}) \text{ and}$$

$$\sum_j q_j PVBP_j^i = PVBP_{\text{Liabilities}}^i$$

Describe what you have done, and the key steps leading to your estimated portfolio.

Part II

Simple Random Cash Flows

Many interest rate derivatives such as interest rate caps or bond options require specific interest rate models for valuation and hedging. Such models are explored in the third part of this book. However, some apparently complex interest rate derivatives are quite easy to analyse without interest rate models. Forwards and futures, floating rate notes and inverse floaters, and generic interest rate swaps can all be analysed using fairly simple 'model-free' techniques.

The key to the valuation and hedging of these instruments, is the replication of the derivative's payoffs through simple strategies such as buying and selling different bonds at different times. From the Law of One Price, if a cash flow can be replicated then it can be valued. Chapter 3 focuses on the US T-bill market, and the associated T-bill futures contracts. Chapter 4 examines the Eurodollar market, floating rate notes, and simple interest rate swaps.

The fact that these instruments can be replicated using simple strategies implies that there is often more than one way of achieving a desired cash flow. The size of transaction costs in the various markets then becomes vital in deciding the cheapest way to achieve one's desired cash flow. A quasi-arbitrage is said to exist when a particular cash flow, can be obtained more cheaply through an indirect path than via the direct approach. We examine transactions costs and their effects on pricing in some detail.

Chapter 3

Forward rates, T-bill futures, and quasi-arbitrage

This chapter is concerned with US Treasury bill market and the T-bill futures contract. We start however, with the basic definition of a forward contract, and the no-arbitrage pricing relation for forward contracts.

3.1 Forward contracts

A *forward contract* is an agreement in which one party contracts today to buy an asset or commodity from another party at a specified future date for a price agreed upon today. With a forward contract payment and delivery occur at the future date. No exchange of money occurs before delivery.

Forward contracts exist on many types of assets, but we shall examine forward contracts on fixed income securities. Specifically, we consider a forward contract where the buyer agrees to buy in 90 days a $1M face value T-bill which matures in another 90 days (i.e. 180 days from today) at a price of 98 cents per dollar of face value. 0.98 is the forward price. This is the price agreed today (time 0) for delivery of a bill at T which matures at $T + 0.25$. This forward contract specifies:

1. **Asset to be exchanged for cash:** $1 million face value of 90-day T-bills.

2. **Date at which exchange takes place:** 90 days from today (time T).

3. **Price:** $0.98 per dollar of face value.

The question we face, is of deciding whether the forward price of $0.98 is good value or not. We shall use an approach based on replication to examine this question.

3.1.1   Replication

The basis of the replication approach is to replicate the payoff of a forward contracts using a portfolio of marketed securities. If payoffs are replicated then the cost of the replicating portfolio must equal the cost of the forward contact.

First we must accurately describe the payoffs to the forward contract. We denote in 3 months time the forward price for the above contract as F_0. Now as of today, the price of a 90 day bill is unknown or random. In our notation this value is $B(0.25, 0.5)$ million.

Today, no cash flows occur. A forward contract to *buy* (a *long* position) requires that, at settlement (in 3 months), we pay the fixed amount $F_0 B(0.25, 0.5)$m and we take delivery of a 90 day bill, which we can immediately sell and receive the prevailing T-bill price $B(0.25, 0.5)$m. Thus the cash flow at settlement (date T) is simply the difference between the prevailing T-bill price and the agreed upon (at date 0) forward price

$$B(0.25, 0.5) - F_0$$

million dollars.

Since we have immediately sold the bill that was delivered to us, and we have no further obligations, there are no cashflows associated with the forward contract, at the maturity date of the T-bill (in 6 months time).

The result is that the forward contract has payoffs consisting of a single random cash flow at settlement in 3 months of the amount shown above. What is the *value* of this cash flow? Since this cash flow can be acquired at zero cost (the forward contract costs nothing to enter) the value of this cash flow is zero. Valuation of a forward contract consists of finding the forward price F_0 such that the payoff from a forward contract has zero value.

We now replicate the above cash flow using marketed securities. In order to receive the random amount $B(0.25, 0.5)$ in 3 months we can simply buy a 6 month bill today. In 3 months time the 6 month bill will be a 3 month bill, and if we sell it we will have a cash inflow of $B(0.25, 0.5)$. The cost today is simply the price of a 6 month bill today $B(0, 0.5)$.

Table 3.1 Replication of a long position in a T-bill forward contract

Date	0	0.25 years
Forward		$B(0.25, 0.5) - F_0$
Replicat. Strat.		
Buy 6 m T-bill	$-B(0, 0.5)$	
sell in 3 months		$B(0.25, 0.5)$
Borrow cash	$B(0, 0.5)$	$-F_0$
Total	$B(0, 0.25)F_0 - B(0, 0.5)$	$B(0.25, 0.5) - F_0$

To create a certain cash outflow of F_0 in 3 months, we simply borrow today for 3 months the present value of this amount. We then have to pay F_0 back in 3 months.

All of this can be shown in a *payoff table*.

The cost at time t of implementing the replicating strategy is

$$B(0, 0.25)F_0 - B(0, 0.5)$$

The Law of One Price implies that this cost must equal the cost of entering the actual forward contract, which is zero. Hence we have derived the forward pricing relation:

$$F_0 = \frac{B(0, 0.5)}{B(0, 0.25)}$$

A particularly simple way to see the relation between bill prices and the forward price of a bill is shown in Figure 3.1.

Each arrow shows the cost in terms of dollars at the date at the tail of the arrow for receiving a dollar at the head of the arrow. Thus as usual $B(t, T)$ and $B(t, T+j)$ show the cost today (date t) for a dollar promised at T and

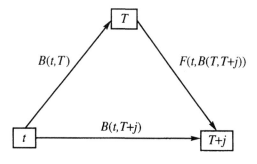

Figure 3.1 T-bills and forward contracts

Table 3.2 Replication of a long-dated T-bill via a short dated T-bill and a forward

Buy	t	T	$T+j$
$T+j$-maturity bill	$-B(t,T+j)$	0	1
Replicating strategy Buy			
Forward contract		$-F(t,B(T,T+j))$	1
T-maturity bills	$-F(t,B(T,T+j))B(t,T)$	$F(t,B(T,T+j))$	
Total from strategy	$-F(t,B(T,T+j))B(t,T)$	0	1

$T+j$ respectively. $F(t,B(T,T+j))$ shows the cost in terms of dollars at time T for receiving a dollar at $T+j$, where the cost is known, i.e. fixed at date t.

The diagram shows how a forward construct in conjunction with a shorter maturity bill replicates a longer maturity bill. Replication involves entering into a forward contract in order to buy a bill at T and thus receive a dollar at $T+j$. This involves us paying $F(t,B(T,T+j))$ at T and to ensure we have the time T dollars to do this we can buy the amount $F(t,B(T,T+j))$ of bills maturing at T.

The trick is to note that the total cost is simply given by multiplying along the arrows. Thus the cost along the bottom arrow is $B(t,T+j)$ and the cost along the upper two arrows is $B(t,T) \times F(t,B(T,T+j))$. The other way to see this relationship is to write out a cash flow diagram as shown in Table 3.2.

Note that here when we take delivery of the bill on the forward contract, we do not sell the bill, but hold it until maturity at $T+j$. As we have assumed that the market for these claims is competitive we know that the Law of One Price holds. This means that the costs of achieving the cash flow of one dollar at time T must be identical for both strategies. This then implies that

$$B(t,T+j) = F(t,B(T,T+j)) \times B(t,T)$$

$$F(t,B(T,T+j)) = \frac{B(t,T+j)}{B(t,T)} \tag{3.1}$$

3.1.2 Forward rates

Although the relation between the spot curve and forwards is most simply expressed in terms of *prices* (as in the above formula), the relationship is more commonly expressed in terms of *rates*. For simplicity, we rewrite the forward pricing relation with the current date as 0:

$$F(0, B(t, T)) = \frac{B(0, T)}{B(0, t)}$$

We now express this relation in terms of rates. For continuously compounded rates, recall that

$$B(0, t) = \exp(-t \cdot r_t)$$

where r_t is the continuously compounded spot rate corresponding to the zero maturing at t. We denote the forward rate corresponding to a loan starting at t with repayment at T, by $f_{t,T}$. The relation between forward rates and forward prices is

$$F(0, B(t, T)) = \exp(-(T - t) \cdot f_{t,T})$$

We can now express the forward pricing equation (3.1) in terms of rates

$$\exp(-(T - t) \cdot f_{t,T}) = \frac{\exp(-T \cdot r_T)}{\exp(-t \cdot r_t)}$$

$$= \exp(-T \cdot r_T + t \cdot r_t)$$

Taking logs on both sides and then dividing by $-(T - t)$ gives:

$$f_{t,T} = \frac{T \cdot r_T - t \cdot r_t}{T - t}$$

Forward rates have a useful interpretation as a *breakeven* rate; reinvestment of the proceeds from a shorter maturity bond at the forward rate results in the same return as investment in the longer maturity bond.

For example assume (annually compounded) the 1 year rate is 10% p.a. and the 2 year rate is 12% p.a. The 1 year forward rate in the second year is the rate which when combined with today's 1 year rate produces the same return as investment over 2 years at the 2 year rate, i.e.

$$1.10 \times (1 + f) = (1.12)^2$$

$$f = \frac{(1.12)^2}{1.10} - 1$$

$$= 14.04\%$$

3.2   T-bill futures

In fact there is no actively traded contract that corresponds exactly to the forward contract as described above. However the specification of the T-bill futures contract is such that it makes payments that enable one to 'lock-in' a certain price for the purchase of a T-bill at a specified future date. Thus a futures contract is similar to a forward contract, in that it enables the determination of a certain price for future delivery of a commodity.

We then examine how futures contracts can be used to lengthen the maturity of a position, and how a 'futures strip' can be used to replicate the payoff of a long-dated zero-coupon bond. This enables the calculation of a spot rate curve from T-bill futures contracts.

3.2.1   Contract specification

Recall that a US Treasury bill is a particularly simple fixed income security. A T-bill has no coupons and simply pays a single cash flow at maturity equal to the face value of the bill which is usually $US1 million. Regular auctions occur on a weekly basis so that there are T-bills expiring every week. The quoted yield is on a discount basis, so that the price is given as

$$\text{T-Bill Price} = \$1\,000\,000 \left(1 - \frac{\text{discount} \times \#\text{days}}{360} \right)$$

The 3-month T-bill futures contract has the following features:

1. **Underlying:** The 3 month T-bill futures contract calls for delivery of a 3 month (often 91 days) US T-bill with face value of $1 million.

2. **Delivery dates:** The contract's delivery days are the Thursday, Friday, and Monday following the third Monday of the contract month.

3. **Quotation:** The T-bill futures price 'Fut' is quoted as 100.00 minus the annual discount expected on the 3 month T-bills to be delivered on the contract.

4. **Invoice price:** The invoice price that must be paid to take delivery of the T-bill at expiration is

$$\$ \left[1 - \frac{100 - \text{Fut}_{\text{expiration}}}{400} \right] \text{m}$$

Like all futures contracts, the T-bill contract involves payments throughout the life of the contract. We denote the futures price quotation today (date t) of a T-bill futures contract maturing at date T by Fut $(t, B(T, T + 0.25))$. This daily payment, called *settlement variation* is specified as \$2500 times the change in futures price from one day to the next, i.e.

$$\$2500 \times [\text{Fut}(t, B(T, T + 0.25)) - \text{Fut}(t - 1_{\text{day}}, B(T, T + 0.25))]$$

Analysis is made much simpler, and at a very low cost in terms of accuracy, if we instead assume that all the payments are made at the expiration date. The contract specifies this payment as

$$\$2500 \times (\text{Futures price at expiration} - \text{Futures price at entry})$$

Thus if a futures contract was 'bought' at 96.00 and the futures was sold at expiration for 96.50 the profit earned would have been \$1250.

At expiration, the absence of arbitrage requires that the cost of purchasing a T-bill via taking delivery on a futures contract equal the cost of purchase of a T-bill in the spot market. This implies that at expiration the futures implied discount $(100 - \text{Fut}_{\text{expiration}})/400$ equal the prevailing discount on 90 day T-bills

$$\frac{(100 - \text{Fut}_{\text{expiration}})}{400} = 90 \text{ day T-bill discount}$$

3.2.2   Using futures contracts to lock in a bill price

Recall that for a 90 day T-bill the relation between price and discount is as follows:

$$\text{T-bill Price} = \$1\,000\,000 \left(1 - \frac{\text{discount}}{4}\right)$$

where the *discount* is expressed in decimal form. We can rewrite this expression as at date T:

$$B(T, T + 0.25) = 1 - \frac{\text{discount}}{4}$$

$$\text{discount} = 4(1 - B(T, T + 0.25))$$

At expiration the futures price is given from the discount on the 3 month bill:

$$\mathrm{Fut}(T, B(T, T+0.25)) = 100 - (100 \times \mathrm{discount})$$
$$= 100 - 400(1 - B(T, T+0.25))$$
$$= -300 + 400B(T, T+0.25)$$

If we enter a futures contract at a price of $\mathrm{Fut}(t, B(T, T+0.25))$ and then buy a bill at the expiration of the contract, the amount we pay is:

contract payoff:$2500 $\times (-300 + 400B(T, T+0.25) - \mathrm{Fut}(t, B(T, T+0.25)))$
    cost of bill:$-\$B(T, T+0.25)$ million
        Total:$2500 $\times (-300 - \mathrm{Fut}(t, B(T, T+0.25)))$

And this amount is fixed as of date t. Thus by purchasing a T-bill futures contract we can lock in a purchase price for a T-bill of

$$\$2500 \times (300 + \mathrm{Fut}(t, B(T, T+0.25)))$$

Furthermore we can solve for the discount that this cost implies:

$$2500 \times (300 + \mathrm{Fut}(t, B(T, T+0.25))) = \$1\,000\,000 \left(1 - \frac{\mathrm{discount}}{4}\right)$$
$$\mathrm{Discount} = 100 - \mathrm{Fut}(t, B(T, T+0.25))$$

Thus we have been able to lock in a price for the T-bill that corresponds to a discount rate, that is exactly equal to the discount rate implied by the futures price when we entered it.

Example 8 *A long position in the March 3 month T-bill futures contract is entered at 94.00 on 2 January. On the last trading date, the futures contract is sold at 96.00 resulting in a received payment of $5000 = \$25 \times 200$ bp. The price of 3 month T-bills which are trading at a discount of 4.00% is*

$$\textit{T-bill price} = \$1\,000\,000 - 1\,000\,000 \times (0.04) \times \left(\tfrac{1}{4}\right)$$
$$= \$990\,000$$

However when you take off from this price the $5000 earned on the futures contract, the result is an effective purchase price of $985\,000 which corresponds *to a discount of 6.0%:*

$$985\,000 = \$1\,000\,000 - 1\,000\,000 \times (0.06) \times \left(\tfrac{1}{4}\right)$$

$$= 1\,000\,000 - 15\,000$$

Instead of using the quoted futures price 'Fut', from now on, we shall use the implied purchase price for a T-bill per unit of face value. The relationship is as follows

$$F(t, B(T, T+0.25)) = 1 - \frac{100 - \text{Fut}(t, B(T, T+0.25))^*}{400}$$

3.2.3   Using T-bill futures contracts to lengthen maturity

Assume that today (date t) we own a T-bill that will mature at date T. We wish to extend the duration of our position, so that the effective maturity of our position is at date $T + 0.25$. One way to do this that does not require selling the original bill is to enter into a futures contract. Denote the futures implied purchase price from the 3 month T-bill contract expiring at T by $F(t, B(T, T+0.25))$. If we enter

$$\frac{1}{F(t, B(T, T+0.25))}$$

long positions in these T-bill futures we shall be able to invest the full face value (\$1 million) of our current bill when it matures at T into new 3 month bills at a known price today of $\$F(t, B(T, T+0.25))$ per dollar face value. The result is that at date $T + 0.25$ we receive the fixed amount

$$\$\frac{1}{F(t, B(T, T+0.25))} \text{ million}$$

and we have in effect extended the duration of our position by 3 months through purchase of a futures contract.

3.2.4   Zero prices from futures prices

We can apply exactly the same reasoning as used above to replicate a 9 month or longer bill. Say we wish to replicate a payment of \$1 million at date T using only 3 month T-bills and a 'strip' of T-bill futures. We have seen that by buying a T-bill futures contract we can lock in a price for buying a T-bill at a future date. Lets call this price $F(0, B(T, T+0.25))$.

The way to approach this problem is to start at the end and work backwards. We know that 3 months prior to T we will want to purchase one 3 month T-bill. This price is unknown now, but if we buy one $T-0.25$ T-bill futures contract we will have locked in an effective purchase price of $\$F(0, B(T-0.25, T))$ million. To have this sum available at $T-0.25$ we will need at $T-0.5$ to have purchased slightly less than one T-bill. At $T-0.5$ we will need to purchase a quantity $F(0, B(T-0.25, T))$ of T-bills. Again the price of the bills will be uncertain but we can hedge by buying the exact same amount of futures contracts $F(0, B(T-0.25, T))$ as bills. This locks in a purchase price of $\$F(0, B(T-0.5, T-0.25))$ million. The amount of cash required at $T-0.5$ therefore is

$$\text{Forward T-bill price} \times \text{quantity}$$

$$= \$F(0, B(T-0.5, T-0.25)) \times F(0, B(T-0.25, T)) \text{ m}$$

We therefore need to purchase this quantity $F(0, B(T-0.5, T-0.25)) \times F(0, B(T-0.25, T))$ of T-bills at $T-0.75$ at an effective price of $F(0, B(T-0.75, T-0.5))$ which is secured by buying $F(0, B(T-0.5, T-0.25)) \times F(0, B(T-0.25, T))$ of T-bill futures expiring at $T-0.5$. Continuing this logic we arrive back to today time 0 where we will need to purchase

$$F(0, B(0.25, 0.5)) \times F(0, B(0.5, 0.75)) \times \cdots \times F(0, B(T-0.25, T))$$

T-bills for a total cost of

$$B(0, 0.25) \times F(0, B(0.25, 0.5)) \times F(0, B(0.5, 0.75)) \times \cdots$$
$$\times F(0, B(T-0.25, T))$$

Rolling over T-bills in this manner will result in a single net cash flow of $\$1$ million at date T, and we have thus replicated a long-dated zero using a T-bill strip. The Law of One Price then implies that the price of the replicating strategy must equal the price of the zero resulting in an arbitrage-free pricing relationship

$$B(0, T) = B(0, 0.25) \times F(0, B(0.25, 0.5)) \times F(0, B(0.5, 0.75)) \times \cdots$$
$$\times F(0, B(T-0.25, T))$$

This analysis simplifies from reality in two ways. First we have assumed away timing problems. In reality we are unlikely to be precisely 3 months away from the next maturing futures contract This problem is easily dealt with. If the next futures contract expires in say 2 months we simply buy a T-bill that will mature then. We thus would purchase a 2 month T-bill at a price of $B(0, 2/12)$.

The second departure from reality is the assumption that the futures contract can be modelled as if it were a forward contract making a solitary payment at expiration. Incorporation of the fact that futures contracts make daily payments is done via a device known as 'tailing'.

3.2.5   Tailing and marking to market

Our analysis so far has treated the payoffs from futures contracts as equivalent to the payoffs of forward contracts. In fact, futures contracts make interim payments, whereas a forward makes a single payment at expiration. This feature makes very little difference to the pricing relations we have derived but it does necessitate an adjustment to the hedging procedures discussed above. This adjustment is called *tailing* and its purpose is to mitigate the effects of interim cash flows from futures contracts.

We now need to change notation slightly. The current date will be called date t rather than 0 as previously, as we want to analyse what happens as time passes by. Suppose that you wish to purchase a T-bill at a future date T, and you hedge today (date t) by buying a T-bill futures contract expiring at T with an implied forward price of $F(t, B(T, T+0.25))$ where the t refers to the current date and the 0.25 refers to the 3 month period. The cash flow that will be received tomorrow $(t+1)$ is

$$\$F(t+1/365, B(T, T+0.25)) - F(t, B(T, T+0.25)) \text{ m}$$

Previously we assumed that this amount was received at T but the actual amount received at T will be the amount that the above grows to when invested. Assuming equal borrowing and lending rates the actual amount received at T due to the price move from today to tomorrow is

$$\$(F(t+1/365, B(T, T+0.25)) - F(t, B(T, T+0.25)))/B(t+1/365, T) \text{ m}$$

As this amount is greater than the first expression we have over-hedged by buying one futures contract to buy one T-bill. Instead we should buy slightly less than one contract. The exact number of contracts to be held at t is

$$\# \text{ Futures contracts} = \# \text{ Forward contracts} \times B(t, T)$$

For every forward contract we would have bought (sold) we buy (sell) less than one futures contract. Note that we now need to adjust the number of futures positions as we approach maturity. As we approach maturity so that t approaches T, $B(t, T)$ approaches 1 and the number of futures contracts approaches the number of forward contracts.

A direct implication of this reasoning results in some simplification of the hedging strategy for replication of a long-dated zero. Recall that in the above analysis the number of contracts increased with the expiration date of the contract, reflecting the fact that as we rolled over T-bills the total number of T-bills bought would increase with time. Recognizing that we are buying futures not forwards, results in buying exactly the same number of futures contracts for all maturities, at any given point in time, but as time passes we need to increase the number of all contracts held.

3.3 Repurchase agreements — 'repos'

An increasingly important component of many interest rate markets is the market for repurchase agreements. The most developed market in repurchase agreements is that associated with the T-bill and T-bill futures markets.

In a *repurchase agreement* or 'repo' one party agrees to sell a security (a T-bill in this case) to another party at one price and also agrees to buy the security back at another price at a future date. The buyer in this arrangement is said to enter a 'reverse repo'.

In effect, the repo market is a market in *collateralized loans*: by putting up a T-bill as security one can borrow money, when you pay the money (plus interest) back the collateral is returned. The interest rate is determined by the difference between the initial sale price and the repurchase price of the security. The rate in a repo is a borrowing rate and is known as the repo rate. The repurchase and sales prices in a repo are related by

$$\text{repurchase price} = \text{sale price} \times \left(1 + \frac{\#\text{days} \times R_p}{360}\right)$$

where R_p denotes the annualized overnight repo rate, and where #days is the length (in days) of the repurchase agreement.

The buyer of a reverse repo is in effect lending money so the *reverse repo rate* is a lending rate. The repo market is a competitive dealer market, with a spread between borrowing and lending rates. This means that repo rates (borrowing rates) are higher then reverse repo rates (lending rates).

Most repos are only for one day, but longer repos exist. Repo agreements that extend for at least 30 days are referred to as *term repos*.

3.3.1   Cash-and-carry with T-bills and repos

Suppose that on 10 June an arbitrager observes the following prices:

- The ask discount on a 100 day T-bill that expires on 20 September is 8.00%.
- The price on June T-bill futures that expires on 20 June is 92.20.
- The repo rate for 10 days is 9.00%.

The arbitrage strategy consists of buying the 100 day bill and then delivering it on the futures contract. In order to finance the purchase of the bill, money is borrowed on the repo market using the bill as collateral.

The exact steps are:

1. Buy a 100 day bill on 10 June for a price of

$$B(0, 100/365) = \$1\,000\,000 \times \left(1 - \frac{0.08 \times 100}{360}\right)$$

$$= \$977\,780$$

2. Short the June futures contract. The locked-in T-bill price for 20 June is

$$F(0, B(10/365, 100/365)) = \$1\,000\,000 \times \left(1 - \frac{(100 - 92.20)}{100}\frac{91}{360}\right)$$

$$= \$980\,280$$

3. Borrow on the repo market for 10 days at 9.00%. This will involve paying back on 20 June the sum:

$$\$977\,780 \times \left(1 + \frac{0.09 \times 10}{360}\right)$$

$$= \$9\,80\,220$$

This series of transactions results in zero cost today, and a payment of $60 = \$980\,280 - 9\,80\,220$ that is certain in 10 days time.

3.3.2 Reverse cash-and-carry with T-bills and reverse repos

Now consider the following set of prices on 10 June:

- The bid discount on a 190 day bill that expires on 20 December is 8.25%.
- The price on T-bill futures that expire on 20 September is 92.30.
- The reverse repo rate is 9.15%.

In order to implement the arbitrage, the following steps are taken:

1. Enter a reverse term repo for 100 days. This involves paying today the price of the 190 day T-bill and receiving the 190 day T-bill. The T-bill's price is

$$B(0, 190/365) = \$1\,000\,000 \times \left(1 - \frac{0.0825 \times 190}{360}\right)$$

$$= \$956\,460$$

on 20 September you will receive back the sum

$$\$956\,460 \times \left(1 + \frac{0.0915 \times 100}{360}\right)$$

$$= \$980\,770$$

2. Immediately sell the 190 day T-bill for its bid price of $956\,460.
3. Enter a long futures position in the September T-bill contract. This locks-in a purchase price on 20 September for a 90 day T-bill of

$$F(0, B(100/365, 190/365)) = \$1\,000\,000 \times \left(1 - \frac{(100 - 92.30)}{100}\frac{90}{360}\right)$$

$$= \$980\,750$$

This set of transactions involves zero net cash flows on 10 June. On 20 September, you receive the sum of $980\,770 from the reverse repo. You then take delivery of the 90 day T-bill on the futures contract, paying \$980 750 for the T-bill, which you then deliver as your part of the reverse repo. Final profit is thus \$20.00.

3.4   Transaction costs and quasi-arbitrage

If futures contracts are effectively equivalent to forward contracts and forward contracts can be created by trading in zero-coupon bonds, it is natural to ask why futures markets are so spectacularly successful. Indeed the language of finance theory suggests this question when it labels a futures contract a *redundant* security in the sense that its payoffs can be replicated by other securities.

The answer is that in a competitive market there would be no role for futures contracts as they would indeed be redundant. However the real world falls short of the competitive ideal. We mentioned previously two areas in which reality departs from the competitive ideal. One is the presence of transaction costs and the other was the role of the enforcement of contracts. We shall see that both are important in understanding the role and pricing of futures contracts.

The analysis presented here closely follows the paper of Kamara (1988). We first introduce some notation. As all prices are going to be set today we dispense with the usual first argument of zero. Thus we define

- $B^A(T)\mathbf{t}_T$: The cost of buying a bill paying one dollar at T, where $B^A(T)$ is the ask price of the security and $\mathbf{t}_T$ is one plus the transaction cost (e.g. search costs, processing, etc.).

- $B^B(T)/\mathbf{t}_T$: The net proceeds from selling a bill paying one dollar at T, where $B^B(T)$ is the asset's current bid price.

- $F(B(T, T+0.25))\mathbf{t}_F$: The cost in time T dollars locked in by the current futures contract for a 3 month bill, where $F(B(T, T+0.25))$ is related to the quoted futures price by the equation marked* on p. 49, and $\mathbf{t}_F$ is one plus the transaction cost associated with operating in the futures market.

- $F(B(T, T+0.25))/\mathbf{t}_F$: The proceeds in time T dollars locked in by the current futures contract for the sale of a 3 month bill.

The above sales prices are predicated on the basis that we own the bill. In a competitive market, in which enforcement is not an issue, the proceeds from selling bills are the same as from shorting them, i.e. that is selling bills when we do not own them. In reality selling something one does not own leaves the counterparty subject to the risk that one will not honour the commitment implied by such an action — namely that the bill will be paid off when due or bought back. Accordingly an extra charge is levied for selling bills that one does not own:

- $B^B(T)/\mathbf{t}_T d_T$: The net proceeds from selling a bill paying one dollar at T, where d_T is one plus a charge for short-selling the asset.

We can now redo the triangle diagram to take account of transaction costs. We first show the triangle for buying in Figure 3.2.

Next we show the triangle for short-selling in Figure 3.3. This figure needs some explanation. The key point is that the quantities appearing beside the arrows represent the cost in terms of dollars at the tail of the arrow for generating one dollar at the head of the arrow. Thus if the proceeds from

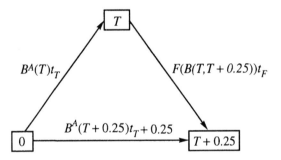

Figure 3.2 Buying bills and futures. Labels refer to the cost of receiving one dollar at the arrow head in terms of dollars at the arrow tail

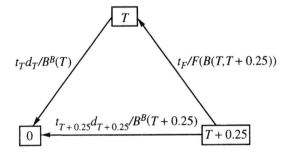

Figure 3.3 Selling T-bills and futures

shorting a bill paying a dollar at T are $B^B(T)/t_T d_T$ we take the inverse of this to get the cost in terms of date T dollars for getting one current dollar.

In order to derive pricing restrictions we need to introduce the concept of quasi-arbitrage or one-way arbitrage. For example in Figure 3.2 we can see that there are two ways to achieve a cash flow of one dollar at date $T + 0.25$: a direct way in which a $(T + 0.25)$-maturity bill is bought and an indirect way in which T-maturity bills are bought and a futures contract is bought. Both ways achieve the same result but at different costs. A one-way arbitrage is said to exist if the indirect way is cheaper than the direct way. This differs from direct arbitrage which requires the creation of a riskless, and also *costless* positive cash flow. The idea behind one-way arbitrage is that a situation of one-way arbitrage cannot be an equilibrium, even though there may be no true arbitrage opportunities. Why not? If the indirect way was cheaper either for buying or selling then the direct market would dry up and cease to function. If we observe a market in existence then this implies an absence of one-way arbitrage and this results in price restrictions that are stronger than the restrictions resulting from the absence of standard arbitrage (after accounting for transactions costs).

Let's examine some of these restrictions.

The market in $(T + 0.25)$-maturity bills

The price restriction for buying is simply that the direct cost of purchasing is less than the indirect cost of purchasing. Now the triangle diagram makes it simple to calculate the costs of various strategies. Simply follow along the arrows and multiply the costs. Thus the direct cost of achieving a dollar at $T + 0.25$ is

$$B^A(T + 0.25)\mathbf{t}_{T+0.25}$$

and the indirect cost is

$$B^A(T)\mathbf{t}_T F(B(T, T + 0.25))\mathbf{t}_F$$

Thus we have the restriction that

$$B^A(T + 0.25)\mathbf{t}_{T+0.25} \leq B^A(T)\mathbf{t}_T F(B(T, T + 0.25))\mathbf{t}_F$$

Now empirical evidence on transactions costs suggests that

$$\mathbf{t}_{T+0.25} \geq \mathbf{t}_T \mathbf{t}_F$$

that is, that the transaction costs associated with longer-term bills are greater than the transaction costs associated with shorter-term bills. This then implies that

$$F(B(T, T + 0.25)) \geq \frac{B^A(T + 0.25)}{B^A(T)}$$

What about selling a $(T + 0.25)$-maturity bill? The costs (in terms of dollars at $T + 0.25$ for a dollar today) is given by following the arrows and multiplying in Figure 3.3. The direct cost of a sale given we already own it is

$$\frac{\mathbf{t}_{T+0.25}}{B^B(T + 0.25)}$$

and the indirect cost is

$$\frac{\mathbf{t}_F \mathbf{t}_T d_T}{B^B(T) F(B(T, T + 0.25))}$$

and the restriction is that costs of direct selling should be less than costs of indirect selling:

$$\frac{\mathbf{t}_{T+0.25}}{B^B(T + 0.25)} \leq \frac{\mathbf{t}_F \mathbf{t}_T d_T}{B^B(T) F(B(T, T + 0.25))}$$

Given our previous assumption on transaction costs this implies that

$$F(B(T, T + 0.25)) \leq \frac{B^B(T + 0.25) d_T}{B^B(T)}$$

This places an upper bound on the futures price but given that costs of short-selling may be reasonably high this bound may not be very constraining.

The market in *T*-maturity bills

By combining the arrows from Figures 3.2 and 3.3 we can easily derive the one-way arbitrage restriction for buying the T-maturity bill:

$$B^A(T)\mathbf{t}_T \leq \frac{B^A(T + 0.25)\mathbf{t}_{T+0.25}\mathbf{t}_F}{F(B(T, T + 0.25))}$$

$$F(B(T, T + 0.25)) \leq \frac{B^A(T + 0.25)\mathbf{t}_{T+0.25}\mathbf{t}_F}{B^A(T)\mathbf{t}_T}$$

and for selling (given we already own it):

$$\frac{t_T}{B^B(T)} \leq \frac{t_{T+0.25}}{B^B(T+0.25)} F(B(T, T+0.25)) t_F$$

$$F(B(T, T+0.25)) \geq \frac{B^B(T+0.25)}{B^B(T)} \frac{t_T}{t_{T+0.25} t_F}$$

The main result from all of this can be summarized quite simply: *the futures price should be above that implied from the ask price of bills.*

3.5 Further reading

Kamara, A. (1988) 'Market Trading Structures and Asset Pricing: Evidence from the Treasury-Bill Markets' *The Review of Financial Studies* 1(4), p. 357–375.

3.6 Questions

1. Suppose that the 9 month interest rate is 6% p.a. (continuous compounding c.c.) and the 6 month interest rate is 5.5% p.a. (c.c.). Estimate the futures price of 90 day T-bills with a face value of $1 million for delivery in 6 months. How is the price quoted?

2. Spot interest rates (annual compounding) are as follows:

Years	Rate (% p.a.)
1	7.0
2	6.5
3	6.2
4	6.0
5	5.9

Calculate forward rates for the second, third, fourth, and fifth years.

3. Spot interest rates (annual compounding) are as follows:

Years	Rate (% p.a.)
1	6.0
2	6.5
3	6.8
4	7.0
5	7.2

Calculate forward rates for the second, third, fourth, and fifth years.

4. The term structure of spot rates (annual compounding) is upward sloping. Rank the following numbers from lowest to highest:

- 3 year spot rate;
- yield on a 3 year coupon bond;
- Forward rate between 3 and $3\frac{1}{2}$ years in the future.

Chapter 4

The Eurodollar market and simple interest rate swaps

A Eurodollar time deposit (TD) is a fixed rate US dollar time deposit in a bank not subject to US banking regulations. The centre of this market is London and there is now over \$3 trillion on deposit. The rate which major money centre banks will lend to each other is called LIBOR — *London Interbank Offer Rate*. LIBOR is an important benchmark borrowing rate and is quoted as an annualized rate assuming 360 days in a year. So if 6 month (180 day) LIBOR is 9%, the interest on \$1 million is

$$\text{Interest} = 0.09 \times \left(\frac{180}{360}\right) \times \$1 \text{ million}$$

In this chapter we examine the major markets associated with Eurodollar deposits — the Eurodollar futures market, the market in forward rate agreements (FRAs), and markets in floating rate notes (FRNs) and simple interest rate swaps. All these instruments can be hedged and valued using the concept of simple replication that was used last chapter for analysing US T-bill futures. We first introduce some notation:

$L(t,T)$: LIBOR rate at time t for a deposit of maturity $T - t$,

$B(t,T)$: Value at t of a dollar delivered at T using LIBOR rates.

There is a spread between LIBOR rates and T-bill rates. The exact cause of this spread is not well understood, and at this stage we follow market convention, and simply assume that LIBOR is the riskless rate for the Eurodollar market. This implies that we can calculate a discount factor $B(t,T)$ using

LIBOR rates, and we shall use this discount factor for discounting all riskless cash flows other than those from US Treasury securities.

4.1   Eurodollar futures

The most widely traded short-term interest rate futures contracts are on Eurodollar time deposit rates. Both LIFFE and the Chicago Mercantile Exchange have Eurodollar contracts. Eurodollar futures contracts are very similar to T-bill futures contracts. At the expiration date (say T) of the Eurodollar futures contract the quoted futures price is given as 100 less the prevailing 3 month LIBOR rate in percentage form:

$$\text{Eurodollar futures price at expiration } T = 100(1 - L(T, T + 0.25))$$

This contract is not deliverable, but is cash settled. The LIBOR rate is taken as an average of selected dealer quotes. Prior to expiration at $t < T$ the quoted futures price provides an implied LIBOR rate that is expected to prevail. We denote this implied future LIBOR rate or forward Libor by $F(t, L(T, T + 0.25))$, where the t tells us today's date when the forward price is being set, and the T and $T + 0.25$ tell us the dates of the loan underlying the rate. We thus have that this implied future LIBOR rate is given from the Eurodollar futures price by:

$$F(t, L(T, T + 0.25)) = 1 - \frac{\text{Eurodollar futures price at } t}{100}$$

Assuming that all gains or losses on a futures contract are realized at expiration, we can write the expiration cash flow as

$$\$2,500 \times (\text{Futures price at expiration} - \text{Futures price at entry})$$

Thus if a futures contract was 'bought' at 96.00 and the futures was sold at expiration for 96.50 the profit earned would have been $1250. We can also write the payoff on a bought Eurodollar futures contract in terms of the change in the implied future Libor rate:

$$\$250\,000 \times (\text{Implied LIBOR rate at entry} - \text{LIBOR at expiration})$$
$$= \$250\,000 \times (F(t, L(T, T + 0.25)) - L(T, T + 0.25))$$

In terms of millions of dollars this can be written as:

$$\$\tfrac{1}{4}(F(t, L(T, T+0.25)) - L(T, T+0.25)) \text{ M}$$

We examine next how we can replicate a long-dated Eurodollar deposit using the 3 month Eurodollar TD market and a strip of Eurodollar futures. We then show how this formula should be adjusted (using a 'tail') for hedging purposes.

4.1.1 Replication of a zero with T-bills and T-bill futures

The analysis of Eurodollar futures contracts is complicated by the fact that the contract is not on a traded security. Instead it is on an interest payment. The way to simplify analysis is to pretend (we shall correct this pretense shortly) that the futures contract pays off not at expiration, but instead 3 months after expiration, at the maturity of the underlying Eurodollar term deposit.

Consider the following replication problem. We wish to replicate the cash flows on a 6 month loan at the 6 month Libor rate, using a 3 month loan and a Eurodollar futures contracts. To be specific we are currently in February and we wish to replicate a 6 month loan maturing in August. As usual we construct a strategy payoff table. We denote the Libor rate in decimal form as $L(t, T)$ where t refers to the current date and T refers to the maturity date of the loan. The first line in Table 4.1 shows the payoff we are trying to replicate, an inward flow today (March) corresponding to a loan of $1 million and an outflow at the maturity of the loan.

The replicating strategy consists of the following:

1. Borrow $1 million on the Eurodollar market for a term of 3 months, and then pay back the principal plus interest in June $\$(1 + \tfrac{1}{4}L(0,3))$ million.

2. Enter a short position of $1 + \tfrac{1}{4}L(0,3)$ in June futures. Although this contract will make daily payments from now till expiration in June pretend the sum of all payments is received in September.

3. In June borrow the sum of money you had to repay on your first loan.

The result is a certain cash outflow in September. To avoid arbitrage this amount must equal the amount available from borrowing in the 6 month loan

Table 4.1 Replication of a 6 month loan via two 3 month loans and a Eurodollar futures position

Date	Mar	June (3)	September (6)
	$M	$M	$M
6 mth loan	1		$-\left(1 + \dfrac{L(0,6)}{2}\right)$

Replicat. strat.			
3 mth loan	1	$-\left(1 + \dfrac{L(0,3)}{4}\right)$	
Sell $1 + \dfrac{L(0,3)}{4}$ Jun futs			$-\left(1 + \dfrac{L(0,3)}{4}\right)\dfrac{(F(0,L(3,6)) - L(3,6))}{4}$
3 month TD		$1 + \dfrac{L(0,3)}{4}$	$-\left(1 + \dfrac{L(0,3)}{4}\right)\left(1 + \dfrac{L(3,6)}{4}\right)$
Total	1	0	$-\left(1 + \dfrac{L(0,3)}{4}\right)\left(1 + \dfrac{F(0,L(3,6))}{4}\right)$

market, thus generating a pricing relation:

$$1 + \frac{180}{360}L(0,6) = \left(1 + \frac{1}{4}L(0,3)\right)\left(1 + \frac{1}{4}F(0,L(3,6))\right)$$

The intuition behind this strategy should be clear. By borrowing short-term and selling Eurodollar futures we can guarantee the rate at which we can 'roll-over' into the second 3 month loan, thus producing a certain cash flow of longer maturity than the original loan.

4.1.2   Zero prices from futures prices

Exactly the same reasoning can be applied to replicate a 9 month or longer loan. Say we wish to replicate a $1 million loan that will mature at date T using only 3 month loans and a 'strip' of Eurodollar futures. The way to approach this problem is opposite from that used with T-bills. With T-bills the *final* payment is known and we work backwards from there. With Eurodollar loans the *initial* amount is known and accordingly we work forwards from the start. We know that 3 months from today we will need to borrow $\$(1 + \frac{1}{4}L(0,3))$. Accordingly we sell $(1 + \frac{1}{4}L(0,3))$ Eurodollar futures contracts expiring in 3 months time. This will lock in an effective interest rate of $F(0, L(3,6))$ resulting in a known payment in 6 months time of

$$\$(1 + \tfrac{1}{4}L(0,3))(1 + \tfrac{1}{4}F(0, L(3,6))) \text{ million}$$

Again we borrow this sum for 3 months and hedge the interest payable by selling $(1 + \frac{1}{4}L(0,3))(1 + \frac{1}{4}F(0, L(3,6)))$ futures expiring in 6 months time. We continue forwards in this manner increasing the number of futures contracts sold as the sum of money owed grows through time. The resultant arbitrage relation is

$$\frac{1}{B(0,T)} = \left(1 + \frac{1}{4}L(0,3)\right)\left(1 + \frac{1}{4}F(0, L(3,6))\right) \times \cdots$$
$$\times \left(1 + \frac{1}{4}F(0, L(T-3,T))\right)$$

where the left-hand side shows the amount that must be repaid from borrowing one dollar for T years, and the right-hand side shows the amount that must be repaid from borrowing and rolling over one dollar in combination with a strip of Eurodollar futures.

4.1.3   Tailing and marking to market

Our analysis so far has been considerably simplified by the fictitious assumption that the payoffs from Eurodollar futures contracts are received 3 months after the expiration of the futures contract, when the underlying TD expires. In fact, futures contracts make interim payments up to expiration of the futures contract. We have seen how an adjustment called *tailing* can allow for the fact that a futures contract differs from a forward contract in that it makes interim payments, and we shall use the same approach here.

Suppose that you wish to borrow $1 million at a future date T, and you sell a T-dated Eurodollar contract at an implied LIBOR rate of $F(t, L(T, T + 0.25))$ to hedge the interest you will have to pay. The cash flow that will be received tomorrow $(t + 1)$ is 0.

$$-\$250\,000 \times (F(t, L(T, T+0.25)) - F(t+1, L(T, T+0.25)))$$

Previously we assumed that this amount was received at $T + 0.25$ but the actual amount received at $T + 0.25$ will be the amount that the above grows to when invested. Assuming equal borrowing and lending rates the actual amount received at $T + 90$ due to the price move from today to tomorrow is

$$-\$250\,000 \times \frac{F(t, L(T, T + 0.25)) - F(t + 1, L(T, T + 0.25))}{B(t + 1, T + 0.25)}$$

As this amount is greater (in absolute value) than the first expression we have over-hedged by buying one futures contract to hedge one million dollars. Instead we should buy slightly less than one contract. The exact amount being

$$\# \text{ Futures contracts held at } t = \# \text{ Original calculation} \times B(t, T + 90)$$

For every contract we would have bought (sold) under the old assumption we now buy (sell) slightly less than one. Note that we now need to adjust the number of futures positions as we approach maturity. As we approach maturity so that t approaches T, $B(t, T + 90)$ approaches $B(T, T + 90)$ the 3 month discount factor. Note therefore that even at maturity we will always hold less futures contracts than under the original calculations.

A direct implication of this reasoning results in some simplification of the hedging strategy for replication of a long-term deposit. Recall that under the original calculation the number of futures contracts held simply equalled the amount that one dollar would have grown to at that date. Thus assuming an initial investment of $1 million at date 0 the number of futures contracts maturing at T that would be held at date t would be

$$\# \text{ Futures contracts (orig. calc)} = \frac{1}{B(t, T)}$$

Under the new calculation the number of date T futures contracts held is

$$\# \text{ Futures contracts held at } t = \frac{B(t, T + 0.25)}{B(t, T)}$$

This is an amount that will be slightly less than one. Furthermore it no longer shows an increasing pattern as produced by the original calculation. An adequate approximation is often obtained by holding the same amount of futures contracts for all maturities:

$$\text{Initial deposit (\$m)} \times \frac{1}{1 + \frac{1}{4} L(0, 0.25)}$$

4.2   Forward rate agreements — FRAs

A forward rate agreement or FRA is an over-the-counter contract in which two parties commit to making a payment at a future date known as the settlement date. The size and direction of the payment depend on the difference between the reference rate for some specified period and the contracted upon rate. A typical dealer quote for an FRA might be 6.45–6.50 for a 4×7, 1-million-Eurodollar FRA. 4×7 means that the settlement date and starting date for the loan underlying the reference rate is in four months time. The loan terminates in 7 months time implying that the reference rate is a 3-month $(7 - 4)$ Eurodollar rate. The contracted rate is 6.50 for a buyer and 6.45 for a seller. The one-off payment payable at the settlement date to a buyer is the present value of the spot borrowing costs less the contracted upon borrowing cost. In our example if at settlement 3 month LIBOR is at 7.05% then the buyer receives the following sum:

$$\left[\frac{1}{1 + 0.0705\left(\frac{90}{360}\right)} \right] \times (0.0705 - 0.0650) \times \frac{90}{360} \times \$10\,000\,000 = \$13\,512$$

This expression is less complex than it looks. The term in the square bracket takes the present value using a simple interest rate convention. The next term is simply the difference in borrowing costs between the prevailing LIBOR rate of 7.05% and the contract rate of 6.50%. Again these costs are calculated using simple interest rates.

Note that a buyer of an FRA stands to profit if rates rise. This is in contrast to most buy positions in the fixed income markets.

The determination of the FRA rate which should prevail in a competitive market is an exercise in the principle of value-additivity. Our goal is to find a strategy which replicates the payoff to an FRA. The cost of this strategy must equal the cost of the FRA and as an FRA is set at inception to have zero cost, so the replicating strategy must have zero cost. For now we assume that we can borrow and lend at LIBOR. A strategy payoff table is shown at Table 4.2. The strategy for using the FRA is as follows:

1. Enter a sell position in a 4×7 \$1-million FRA. The proceeds from this in 4 months will be

$$-\$ \left(\frac{1}{1 + 0.25L(4,7)} \right) 0.25(L(4,7) - \text{ FRA}) \text{ M}$$

where FRA is the negotiated forward rate.

Table 4.2 Replication of an FRA plus deposit

Time (mths)	0	4	7
FRA + deposit	$M	$M	$M
FRA (sell)	0	$-\frac{\frac{1}{4}(L(4,7)-\text{FRA})}{1+\frac{1}{4}L(4,7)}$	0
then deposit		$\frac{\frac{1}{4}(L(4,7)-\text{FRA})}{1+\frac{1}{4}L(4,7)}$	$\frac{-(L(4,7)-\text{FRA})}{4}$
Deposit $1 mill.		-1	$1+\frac{1}{4}L(4,7)$
Total		-1	$1+\frac{1}{4}\text{FRA}$
Replic. strat.			
7 mth deposit	$-B(0,7)\times$ $(1+\frac{1}{4}\text{FRA})$		$1+\frac{1}{4}\text{ FRA}$
Borrow PV of $1m for 4 mth	$B(0,4)$	-1	
Total	$-B(0,7)\times$ $(1+\frac{1}{4}5\text{FRA})$ $+B(0,4)$	-1	$1+\frac{1}{4}\text{ FRA}$

2. Invest this money for 3 months producing a payment in 7 months of $0.25(L(4,7) -$ FRA$)$ million.

3. Invest $1 million in 4 months time for a term of 3 months producing a final cash balance in 7 months of $1 + 0.25L(4,7)$ million.

The upper panel shows that selling an FRA and then depositing cash at the expiration of the FRA results in a locked-in deposit rate equal to the rate contracted for under the FRA. The bottom panel shows how the same payoffs could be achieved by operating in the cash market alone.

1. Deposit the present value of $1 + 0.25$FRA million in a 7 month Eurodollar deposit.

2. Borrow the present value of $1 million for 4 months.

Note that the two strategies have equal payoffs in periods 4 and 7. The Law of One Price, then states that the value today (cost) must be the same. But the FRA deposit strategy has an initial zero cost, so the strategy shown

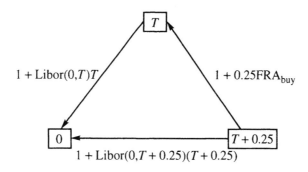

Figure 4.1 Libor and a bought FRA

in the bottom panel must also have a zero cost. This implies

$$0 = B(0,7) \times (1 + 0.25 \times \text{FRA}) - B(0,4)$$

$$\text{FRA} = 4 \times \left(\frac{B(0,4)}{B(0,7)} - 1 \right)$$

Thus the FRA rate that is contracted for will, in the absence of transactions costs, equal the forward rate implied from the zero curve.

Of course in the real world transaction costs will affect the above calculation. We show next how to account for transaction costs. In the Eurodollar markets the deposit rate Libid is typically 0.125 percent below Libor and this is constant for all maturities.

Now consider replicating a sell position in an FRA. Such a position is very similar to a forward contract on a bill, and we can use the triangle diagrams to easily see the effects of bid–ask spreads on one-way arbitrage pricing restrictions.

We examine the one-way arbitrage bounds implied from the existence of an active market in FRAs. For a short FRA position we must have

$$1 + 0.25 \, \text{FRA}_{\text{sell}} \geq \frac{1 + \text{Libid}(0,T)T}{1 + \text{Libor}(0,T+0.25)(T+0.25)}$$

or else a person desiring a short FRA position could construct a better deal in the spot market. We leave as an exercise the analogous expression for a long position in an FRA. Table 4.3 shows these bounds for different start dates. We assume a flat curve, where Libor is at 5.0% and Libid is at 5.125%.

Note that as we extend into the future the arbitrage bounds become very large. At five years the bounds are well over 400 basis points! This shows

Table 4.3 Bounds on FRA rates from LIBOR and LIBID

Start date (months)	FRA(sell)	FRA(buy)
3	4.79	5.14
6	4.67	5.26
12	4.43	5.49
18	4.19	5.72
24	3.94	5.95
36	3.47	6.41
48	2.99	6.88
60	2.51	7.34

not only the difficulty of arbitraging the FRA/Eurodollar market but also shows that FRAs typically provide a much cheaper way of locking in future borrowing or lending rates than by taking direct positions in the Eurodollar market. The cost of transacting in the Eurodollar market also provides strong incentives for the trading of futures on Eurodollars and we now examine this important section of the Eurodollar market.

4.3 Floating rate notes

Floating rate notes (FRNs) are bonds whose coupon payments are not fixed but vary with the level of some interest rate index. In general variable cash flows are more difficult to value than fixed cash flows but some FRNs provide an important exception to this rule. Current time is 0 and there are N coupons to be paid at dates $T_1, T_2, \ldots, T_N$. In general, we can specify a coupon payment as

$$C(T_k) = \text{Index Rate } (T_k - h) + \text{markup}$$

where T_k is the date at which the coupon is paid, $T_k - h$ is the *reset* date for the kth coupon, being the date at which the chosen interest rate index is observed for calculation of the coupon payment. A *markup* over the base rate is often charged in order to issue the bond at par or to account for credit risk.

In this section we only examine 'perfect' floaters. 'Perfect' floaters are defined as having zero markup and zero default risk; the reset date of the next coupon equals the current coupon's date: $T_k - h = T_{k-1}$; and the index rate is the period rate. An example using 6 month LIBOR will make this clear.

Denote the 6 month LIBOR rate at date t by $L(t, T+0.5)$, and denote the zero-coupon curve derived from LIBOR and from Eurodollar futures by $B(0, T)$ being the amount required to deposit today (date 0) to generate one dollar at T. Measuring time in years we immediately have that

$$B(0, 0.5) = \frac{1}{1 + (0.5 \times L(0, 0.5))}$$

where LIBOR L is obviously in decimal form.

Consider an FRN with semi-annual coupons set to the LIBOR rate prevailing 6 months prior. The coupon payment at a date T is given as

$$C(T) = 0.5 \times L(T - 0.5, T)$$

where the 0.5 reflects the fact that coupons are paid semiannually. Another way of expressing this is as

$$C(T) = \frac{1}{B(T - 0.5, T)} - 1$$

For concreteness, assume a 2 year FRN with face value of $1 million. Then the cash flows are as shown in Table 4.4.

Note that the final payment lacks a minus one, due to the repayment of principal ($1 million). To value this FRN, we pursue, our (by now) usual strategy of attempting to replicate the payoffs to it. Consider the following: deposit $1 million in a 6 month Eurodollar TD that pays LIBOR. In

Table 4.4 Cash flows of a 2 year floating rate note

Date (years)	Payment ($m)
0.5	$\frac{1}{B(0, 0.5)} - 1$
1	$\frac{1}{B(0.5, 1)} - 1$
1.5	$\frac{1}{B(1, 1.5)} - 1$
2	$\frac{1}{B(1.5, 2)}$

Table 4.5 2 year perfect floating rate note

Date yrs	0	0.5	1	1.5	2
FRN cash flows	$-x$	$0.5L(0,0.5)$	$0.5L(0.5,1)$	$0.5L(1,1.5)$	$1+0.5L(1.5,2)$

			Replicating strategy		
	-1	$B(0,0.5)^{-1}$			
		-1	$B(0.5,1)^{-1}$		
			-1	$B(1,1.5)^{-1}$	
				-1	$B(1.5,2)^{-1}$
Total	-1	$\dfrac{1}{B(0,0.5)}-1$	$\dfrac{1}{B(0.5,1)}-1$	$\dfrac{1}{B(1,1.5)}-1$	$\dfrac{1}{B(1.5,2)}$

6 months our deposit will have grown to $\$1/B(0,0.5)$ million. Then reinvest not all the money but exactly $1 million in a 6 month Eurodollar TD. The amount left over is $\$1/B(0,0.5)-1$ million corresponding to the coupon payment $C(0.5)$ of the FRN. At date 1 we receive the sum $\$1/B(0.5,1)$ million of which $1 million can be reinvested, etc. Table 4.5 details the complete strategy.

Noting that the coupon payment $0.5L(t,t+0.5)$ exactly equals $B(t,t+0.5)^{-1}-1$, we see that the TOTAL row exactly matches the cash flows of the FRN. Thus by following a simple strategy of reinvestment we can replicate the FRN. The initial cost of the replication strategy is $1 million, or par, so the FRN must have a value x of one million dollars. In fact it is not hard to see that a 'perfect' FRN is always valued at par at ex-coupon dates.

What about the value at intermediate dates? Consider a date t between dates T, and $T+0.5$. We know that after payment of the coupon at $T+0.5$ the FRN will be worth par or $1 million. The actual coupon payment at date $T+0.5$ is known as we are currently past the reset date. Thus we know that at $T+0.5$ the FRN will have a certain value of

$$\$1/B(T,T+0.5) \text{ million}$$

To find the value of this today at time t we simply discount this value back:

$$\$\frac{B(t,T+0.5)}{B(T,T+0.5)} \text{ million}$$

and the price will vary as the current discount factor $B(t,T+0.5)$ varies.

4.4 Simple interest rate swaps

An interest rate swap is an agreement between two parties to exchange streams of cash flows based on a hypothetical (or notional) principal amount when one stream is calculated with reference to a floating rate and the other stream is fixed. In this section we examine the generic fixed for floating interest rate swap. In a fixed for floating swap, the party who has *bought* the swap *pays* a fixed amount (called the swap rate) at each payment date, and receives a variable payment dependent on the level of an interest rate index. Swaps are priced at zero when they are entered into, with the pricing variable being the level of the fixed payment.

An instructive way of looking at a swap is in terms of its two components. The *fixed leg*, which is the set of fixed cash flows plus the principal repayment, is like a standard coupon bond with the coupon level set to the agreed swap rate. The *floating leg* is like a floating rate note. Since we know how to value both these forms of security swap valuation in this case is quite straightforward.

When a swap is entered into it typically has zero value, just as a forward contract when entered into has zero value. Valuation involves finding the fixed coupon rate such that fixed and floating legs have equal value at inception. As we know that a perfect FRN must have value equal to par at inception, we have that the swap rate K on a fixed for floating swap with semi-annual payments must set the fixed rate equal to par. Consider a swap with payment days $t_1, t_2, \ldots, t_N$ set in the terms of the swap. The fixed payment is calculated as

$$\text{Fixed payment at } t_i = (t_i - t_{i-1}) \times \text{Swap rate} \times \text{Principal}$$

Given a set of discount factors at these dates, i.e. $B(0, t_1), B(0, t_2), \ldots, B(0, t_N)$, we can write the value-at-par condition for the fixed leg as

$$1 = B(0, t_N) + \sum_{i=1}^{N} (t_i - t_{i-1}) \times K \times B(0, t_i)$$

$$K = \frac{1 - B(0, t_N)}{\sum_{i=1}^{N} (t_i - t_{i-1}) \times B(0, t_i)}$$

where K is the swap rate. The floating LIBOR-based payment is calculated as

$$\text{Floating payment at } t_i = \frac{1}{B(t_{i-1}, t_i)} - 1$$

The value of a swap though customarily set to zero at inception need not have zero value after inception. The value of a buy position in a swap at some time after inception is given as the difference in value between the floating and fixed legs. Consider the date t between the inception date t_0 and the first payment date t_1. The swap value is then given as

Swap value $(t) =$ Value of floating leg $-$ Value of fixed leg

$$= \left[B(t, t_1) \frac{1}{B(0, t_1)} \right] - \left[B(t, t_N) + K \sum_{i=1}^{N} (t_i - t_{i-1}) \times B(t, t_i) \right]$$

In practice although swaps are derivative securities, they have become so common that the swap rate is used for calculation of spot rates in the Eurodollar market. The formula was given in Equation 1.1 in Section 1.2.3.

4.5   Hedging and PVBP

The goal of hedging is similar to that of immunization. In both cases the aim is to reduce the risk of an *overall* position. Immunization is predicated on the assumption that the overall position can be clearly cut into two portfolios — a given set of liabilities, and a bond portfolio which is chosen to minimize the risk of the overall position. Hedging makes no such assumption as to the composition of liabilities and assets. Instead, hedging involves adding securities to a position so that the resultant position is less risky. The securities added may be assets, liabilities, or zero-cost securities such as futures. The position being hedged may also be an asset, a liability, or a zero-value position such as a swap.

   One of the functions of an investment bank is to act as an intermediary between borrowers and lenders, or more generally between parties with offsetting desired positions. An investment bank might therefore buy or construct a certain position from an outside party, in the expectation that it will find a third party to which the position can be on-sold. If the buyer and seller were both available at the same time, then the bank would be a pure intermediary. Often however this does not happen, and in the period before the offsetting trade can be made, the position can be at substantial risk. The idea of hedging is to add assets or liabilities to the portfolio so as to minimize the risk of the portfolio. No assumptions about the composition of the original position or the added securities is made.

It is important to realize that the concept of duration and key rate duration developed in Chapter 2 is not formally applicable to the above case. This is because duration is defined as the *proportional* change in the value of a position from a change in yield. It presupposes that the position has a value. For any zero-cost position such as a swap or a futures contract duration is undefined. Duration is therefore formally inapplicable for the analysis of hedging. However a related concept, price-value per basis point — PVBP — which is similar to duration can be used instead. PVBP uses the concept of value change in absolute terms rather than relative or proportional terms, and thus bypasses the problems that arise when using duration for zero-value positions. Like duration we look at both single factor versions of PVBP and a multi-factor key rate approach to PVBP.

4.5.1 Price value per basis point

PVBP of a position is simply the change in the position's value associated with a change in the reference yield of 1 basis point (0.01%). This can be calculated for a bond, but unlike duration, it can also be calculated for a zero-value position such as a swap, or a futures position. For example we already know that a T-bill futures position has a PVBP of $25.

For a position consisting of a single instrument PVBP is defined as the price change associated with a 1 basis point change in *own* yield. A simple application of PVBP to hedging is to add positions to the original position such that the resultant PVBP of the overall position is set equal to zero. This strategy implicitly assumes that the yields on all relevant instruments move perfectly together. This assumption is simplistic but results in a very amenable analysis stemming from the fact that PVBP is *additive*. For example say we have bought a 10% 10 year bond which is trading at par, i.e. $1 million. The PVBP of the bond is around $200 so we could hedge it by selling eight T-bill futures. This produces an overall PVBP of zero. In general there will be many different ways of achieving a PVBP of zero. In the above example it may have been possible to short one 10 year Treasury futures contract. This also would have resulted in an overall PVBP of zero. Unfortunately PVBP cannot tell us which of these two strategies provides a better hedge. The assumption that all rates move in unison suggests that anything can be hedged by choosing the appropriate number of any other instrument. This is clearly fallacious so we now introduce a method which results in better actual hedging performance.

4.5.2   Key rates

The essence of the problem with the simplistic use of PVBP as outlined above was the untenable assumption that all rates moved in unison. The key rate approach as outlined in Chapter 2 instead selects a small number of key rates and then assumes that all other rates move in line with these rates.

    The actual formula is quite simple. Say we select as key rates the 1 year, 10 year, and 30 year zero rates. The effect of a move in a key rate on other rates is a linear function of the difference in maturity of the relevant rate from the key rate. For example a 1 bp move in the 1 year rate produces a 1 bp move in the 1 year rate, a zero move in the 10 year rate, and a linear interpolation for all rates in between. Thus the effect on rates diminishes at a rate of 1/9 bp per year of maturity. The 5 year rate thus has a sensitivity to the 1 year rate of

$$1 - (5 - 1) \times \tfrac{1}{9} = 0.56 \text{ bp}$$

With three key rates we now have three PVBPs one for each of the key rates. Hedging strategies are formed by adding positions to the original portfolio such that the all three PVBPs are set equal to zero. To the extent that the key rates adequately capture moves in the yield curve we will have hedged the position against any move in the yield curve not just a parallel shift.

4.6   Questions

1. A bank has 'bought' an interest rate swap in which it agreed to pay fixed 8% p.a. and receive 6 month LIBOR on a notional principal of $100 million, with payments being exchanged every 6 months. The swap has a remaining life of 2 years and 2 months. The current spot curve is flat at 6.0% p.a. (annual compounding). Four months ago the 6 month LIBOR rate was 5.8%. What is the value of the swap today?

Part III

General Rate-Sensitive Cash Flows

This part of the book covers the more complex problems of interest rate derivative pricing. We start by outlining the basic no-arbitrage approach to fixed income, and we then examine several specific 'one-factor' models of interest rates.

Chapter 5

No-arbitrage and risk-neutral pricing

The preceding chapters have shown how a security or derivative can be valued if one can construct a portfolio which replicates the cash flows of the original security. The cost of the replicating portfolio must, by the Law of One Price, be the value of the original security. We have also seen that the presence of transaction costs results in some modification of this principle. But how can one value derivatives such as a bond option? No simple strategy can replicate the payoff on a bond option, so valuation by replication may no longer seem to be appropriate.

In fact the valuation by replication approach is still used for the case of complex interest rate derivatives. Fischer Black and Myron Scholes (1973) showed how (at least in theory) a replicating portfolio could be constructed for a call option on a stock. The price behaviour of bonds is very different from the price behaviour of stocks so we cannot simply use the Black–Scholes option formula. Instead we use their approach of replication. This approach is most easily seen (and implemented on computer) by using a binomial formulation of uncertainty.

5.1 A binomial example — a call option on a 6 month T-bill

Let's assume that the current 6 month and 1 year T-bill rates are 10% on a discount basis. We are interested in pricing a European call option with expiration in 6 months time on the 6 month T-bill. The strike is 95.5 thus

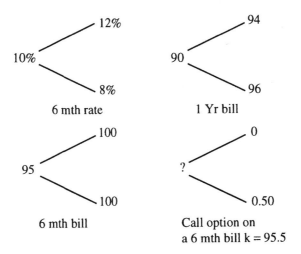

Figure 5.1 A 6 month binomial tree

the option gives the right to buy a 6 month bill for a price of 95.50 in 6 months time. The 6 month bill has a current price of 95.00 and the 1 year bill a price of 90.00. Now let's assume that in 6 months time the 6 month discount will be either 8% or 12%. This corresponds to a binomial tree for the 6 month rate. This information also implies a binomial tree for the 1 year bond. It can go from 90 (today) to either 94 or 96 in 6 months time (by then it will have become a 6 month bill). On the other hand the 6 month bill, which is currently at 95 goes to 100 in both states of the world, i.e. with certainty.

Now it is a surprising fact that in this very simple world we have constructed we can find a unique arbitrage-free price for this call option. On the 6 month bill in 6 months time. For example, lets say the call has a strike of 95.50. The payoff will then either be $0.50 or zero depending on whether the 6 month rate drops to 8% or rises to 12%. Even though we do not know the probability of these occurrences we can price this option. The reason we can do so is that we can replicate the payoff to this option, simply by trading in the 1 year and 6 month bills. Say we buy x of the 6 month bill and y 1 year bills, the payoff in the up-state will be

$$x \cdot 100 + y \cdot 94$$

and the payoff in the down-state will be

$$x \cdot 100 + y \cdot 96$$

To replicate the call we simply need to find x and y that solves the following equations:

$$x \cdot 100 + y \cdot 94 = 0$$
$$x \cdot 100 + y \cdot 96 = 0.5$$

and this is solved for $y = 0.25$ and $x = -0.235$. We thus can replicate this call option by buying 0.25 of a 1 year bill and shorting 0.235 of a 6 month bill, for a total cost of

$$-0.235 \times 95 + 0.25 \times 90 = 0.175$$

Thus the value of the option is \$0.175

Note that we were able to price this option, without regard to the actual probabilities of an up-state or down-state occurring. Furthermore, we could develop a multi-period model and price more complex derivatives by constructing the replicating strategy and finding its cost. However there is an easier way.

5.2   State prices

Recall that when valuing a set of fixed cash flows, we first constructed a set of discount factors. With a complete set of discount factors valuation was simple — just multiply and add. We now employ the same procedure. Instead of calculating discount factors we calculate state prices. A state price, also called an Arrow–Debreu state price, or the price of a primitive security, is the price of a dollar to be delivered in a particular state of the world. A state of the world is simply a node of the tree. In this example there are only two states the up-state (the 'up' refers to interest rates) which we label u and the down-state labelled d. There are thus two A–D securities one paying off \$1 in u and zero in d and the other paying zero in u and \$1 in d. The prices of the two A–D securities are denoted $G(u)$ and $G(d)$. The concept of a state price is very simple, but also highly abstract. These primitive or Arrow–Debreu securities are best thought of as betting tickets that payoff in a particular state of the world. As usual we price them via replication. Thus we find a replicating portfolio (x, y) that pays off one dollar in the down-state, and zero in the up-state:

$$x \cdot 100 + y \cdot 94 = 0$$
$$x \cdot 100 + y \cdot 96 = 1$$

This is solved by $y = 0.5$ and $x = -0.47$ with a resultant cost of 0.35. We thus have that the price of the A–D security paying off in the down-state is

$$G(d) = 0.35$$

Likewise for valuing the A–D security paying off in the up-state. We find the replicating portfolio paying one in the up-state

$$x \cdot 100 + y \cdot 94 = 1$$

$$x \cdot 100 + y \cdot 96 = 0$$

which is solved for $y = -0.5$ and $x = 0.48$ for a price of

$$0.48 \cdot 95 - 0.5 \cdot 90 = 0.60$$

We thus have that the state price for the up-state is $0.60

$$G(u) = 0.60$$

and the state price for the down-state is $0.35. Now the reason that A–D securities are sometimes called primitive securities is that all other securities can be constructed from them. Thus a 6 month note paying $100 with certainty in 6 months time, is formed by buying 100 up-state claims, and 100 down-state claims. Note that the price of this is

$$100(0.60 + 0.35) = \$95$$

which is the price of a 6 month note. In fact with a complete set of state prices any random cash flow can be valued. The formula is simply

$$V = G(d) \times \left(\begin{array}{c} \text{Cash flow in} \\ \text{down state} \end{array} \right) + G(u) \times \left(\begin{array}{c} \text{Cash flow in} \\ \text{up state} \end{array} \right)$$

Let's check that this formula values the call option previously calculated:

$$\text{Value of call} = G(d) \times 0.5 + G(u) \times 0$$

$$= 0.35 \times 0.5$$

$$= 0.175$$

So the call option is correctly valued. There exists a particularly simple and useful relationship between state prices and zero-coupon bond prices. A standard zero-coupon bond pays one dollar at date T with certainty. Certainty, in an uncertain world means that a dollar is paid in each and every state that can occur at date T. We can thus replicate a zero-coupon bond paying at date T by purchasing all the A–D securities that payoff at T. The cost of this replicating strategy must equal the cost of a zero-coupon bond. In our example we show that the sum of the state prices must equal the 6 month discount factor:

$$G(u) + G(d) = 0.60 + 0.35$$

$$= 0.95$$

which does in fact equal the (scaled) price of the 6 month bill.

5.3 Risk-neutral probabilities

We now provide another way of viewing the arbitrage-free approach. Consider pricing by arbitrage a general cash flow $X = (X_u, X_d)$ where X_u is the cash flow in the up-state and X_d is the cash flow in the down-state. We start by finding the replicating portfolio (x, y) consisting of x 6 month bills and y 1 year bills. This will then cost

$$x95 + y90$$

In 6 months time this portfolio will have values of

$$\text{up-state} : x100 + y94$$

$$\text{down-state} : x100 + y96$$

Choosing x and y so that this portfolio perfectly replicates the random cash flow X requires solving

$$x100 + y94 = X_u$$

$$x100 + y96 = X_d$$

Solving these equations we find

$$x = \frac{48}{100}X_u - \frac{47}{100}X_d$$

$$y = \frac{1}{2}X_d - \frac{1}{2}X_u$$

This portfolio has a cost of

$$x95 + y90 = (48X_u - 47X_d)0.95 + (X_d - X_u)45$$

$$= 0.95 \left[\left(48 - \frac{45}{0.95} \right) X_u + \left(-47 + \frac{45}{0.95} \right) X_d \right]$$

This is the solution for the arbitrage-free value of the cash flow X. This solution has a very useful property. We can write it as follows:

$$V(X) = 0.95[p_u X_u + p_d X_d]$$

where

$$p_u = 48 - \frac{45}{0.95}$$

$$p_d = -47 + \frac{45}{0.95}$$

and most importantly

$$p_u + p_d = 1$$

$$p_u > 0$$

$$p_d > 0$$

Thus p_u and p_d have the mathematical interpretation of being probabilities — they are positive and sum to one. The valuation formula can now be given the following interpretation.

The value of the random cash flow X is given as the present value (0.95 is the riskless discount factor) of the expected cash flow X, where the expectation is calculated using the risk-neutral probabilities p_u and p_d.

5.4   Linking state prices and probabilities

Much of modern finance theory utilizes the fact that there is a very close correspondence between state prices and probabilities. This was first pointed out in 1937 by Bruno de Finetti, an Italian probability theorist. What are these similarities? First, state prices like probabilities must lie between zero and one. A state price cannot be worth more than one since a claim to a dollar cannot be worth more than one dollar. A negative state price would imply an arbitrage, receiving something for nothing. The second point of similarity that De Finetti noticed is that just as the probabilities of mutually exclusive events is additive so the prices of claims on mutually exclusive events must also be additive. This simply follows from the Principle of Value Additivity, itself a consequence of no-arbitrage. We shall see that there are deeper parallels between probabilities and state prices, but you may have noticed an important distinction between state prices and probabilities.

This distinction is that the sum of probabilities of all mutually exclusive events must equal one. However we know that the sum of state prices does not equal one, the sum equals the price of a zero or a discount factor which is always less than one. In the above case, the sum of state prices is only equal to 0.95. This point was not recognized by de Finetti, but was addressed by Cox and Ross (1976) and Harrison and Kreps (1978). They showed how state prices could be adjusted so that they could act as probabilities. Not the objective probabilities, or subjective probabilities of anyone in particular, but simply a set of probabilities called risk-neutral probabilities.

The trick they employed was simply to *scale* state prices up so that they summed to one, and hence could act as probabilities. This can be done by multiplying the state price at a future date by the value that one dollar invested at 0 would have grown to invested at the short-term risk-free rate. In the above binomial example one dollar invested in 6 month bills would have grown to $1/0.95$. We thus define the risk-neutral probabilities in the up and down states by

$$\begin{aligned} p(u) &= G(u)/0.95 \\ &= 0.60/0.95 \\ &= 0.6316 \end{aligned}$$

and

$$\begin{aligned} p(d) &= G(d)/0.95 \\ &= 0.35/0.95 \\ &= 0.3684 \end{aligned}$$

First note that the new risk-neutral probability measure p has the essential properties of being positive and summing to one. The reason it is called risk-neutral is because it also has the following property. *All securities have an expected return equal to the risk-free return when the expectation is calculated using risk-neutral probabilities.*

We can prove this result in the following way. We assume that the state price valuation formula is correct and then show that this implies that all securities have expected returns equal to the short rate. So for a security with payoffs X_u in the up-state and X_d in the down-state we have that value V is given by

$$V(X) = X_u G(u) + X_d G(d)$$

Now divide and multiply by 0.95

$$V(X) = 0.95 \left[X_u \frac{G(u)}{0.95} + X_d \frac{G(d)}{0.95} \right]$$

$$= 0.95[X_u \pi_u + X_d \pi_d]$$

$$= 0.95 \times E^p[X]$$

Rearranging this gives

$$\frac{E^p[X]}{V(x)} = \frac{1}{0.95}$$

which states that the expected return is the same as the riskless return.

We can check this for the call option and the 1 year bill. Recall that the option's price was 17.5c and the payoffs were zero and 50c. The expected payoff therefore is

$$E^p[\text{option payoff}] = 0.6316 \times 0 + 0.3684 \times 0.50$$

$$= \$0.1842$$

Dividing this by the initial price of the option gives the gross return

$$\frac{0.1842}{0.175} = 1.0526$$

$$= 1/0.95$$

which is the same return as on the 6 month bill.

Similarly for the 1 year bill we have the expected payoff is

$$p(d) \times 96 + p(u) \times 94 = 0.6316 \times 96 + 0.3684 \times 94$$

$$= 95.263$$

Dividing by the initial price we again see that the expected return is the same as on the 6 month bill:

$$\frac{95.263}{90} = \frac{1}{0.95}$$

5.5   Multi-period valuation

The basic principle of valuation via replication extends simply to a multi-period analysis of the binomial model. The one new tool that is required is the *principle of dynamic programming*. Dynamic programming makes complex multi-period problems easy to solve by decomposing one multi-period problem into a number of one-period problems which can be solved individually. The trick to dynamic programming is that the one-period problems are solved in reverse order through time. That is, we start at the end and work backwards. The next section shows how this approach is used in a three-period binomial tree. We then generalize the approach to an n-period problem.

5.5.1   A three-period binomial model

The purpose of this example is to show how dynamic programming can be combined with a binomial tree for the valuation of derivatives. We shall assume that we have developed a tree which correctly prices all the existing securities. Moreover, in this tree the risk-neutral probabilities of up and down moves are equal at 0.5. In practice one can alter these risk-neutral probabilities to fit observed prices, but the more common procedure is to alter the node values (i.e. the interest rates) rather than the probabilities so as to fit prices. Consider the following annual binomial tree for the 1 year interest rate (annual compounding).

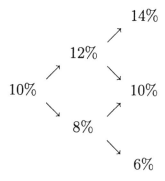

Year 0   Year 1   Year 2

Assuming that the risk-neutral probabilities are 0.5 for up and down moves how can we price for example a 3 year zero-coupon bond? Dynamic programming suggests that we start at the end and work backwards. In *Year 3* we know the 3 year bond will have value equal to its face value which we normalize to 100. In *Year 2* the bond is now a 1 year bond, and since we know the 1 year rates in each of the three states we can calculate the price associated with each of these 1 year rates. The prices of the 3 year bond in years 2 and 3 are thus given by:

$$\frac{100}{1.14} = 87.72 \longrightarrow 100$$

$$\frac{100}{1.10} = 90.91 \longrightarrow 100$$

$$\frac{100}{1.06} = 94.34 \longrightarrow 100$$

Year 2   Year 3

Now the prices in year 1 require a slightly more difficult calculation. Using symbols $x, y,$ and z for the unknown prices of the 3 year bond in years 1 and 0 we can write the price process for the 3 year bond as

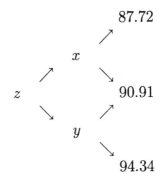

Year 0   Year 1   Year 2

Let us consider finding the value for x—the price in year 1 when the 1 year rate is 12%. To find x we recall that under risk-neutral probabilities all securities have expected returns equal to the risk-free return. The expected return from holding the 3 year bond from the 12% node in year 1 for 1 year is simply

$$\frac{0.5 \times (87.72 + 90.91)}{x}$$

Setting this equal to the known 12% return from holding a 1 year bond gives an equation:

$$1.12 = \frac{0.5 \times (87.72 + 90.91)}{x}$$

Solving this equation results in a value of x of

$$x = \frac{0.5 \times (87.72 + 90.91)}{1.12}$$

$$= 79.75$$

Similarly we can use the same procedure to solve for y:

$$1.08 = \frac{0.5 \times (90.91 + 94.34)}{y}$$

$$y = \frac{0.5 \times (90.91 + 94.34)}{1.08}$$

$$= 85.76$$

The price tree now looks like:

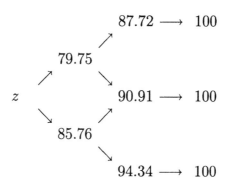

Year 0   Year 1   Year 2   Year 3

With values now obtained for year 1 we can find the year 0 value by again requiring that the 3 year bond have an expected return equal to the known 1 year riskless return of 10%:

$$z = \frac{0.5(79.75 + 85.76)}{1.10}$$

$$= 75.23$$

Thus by starting at the end and applying the one-period risk-neutral pricing result that all securities have expected return equal to the riskless rate, we can work backwards through the tree to provide a value today. This pricing approach is called *backward induction*, and it can be used to value any set of cash flows in the tree not just a zero-coupon bond.

For example, consider a European option to buy in year 2 a 1 year bond with face value of $100 for $90. When interest rates are high (i.e. at the 14% node in year 2) this option is worthless, but at the other two nodes (the 10% and the 6% nodes) the option will have terminal values of $0.91 and $4.34 respectively. To value this option we construct a tree, inserting the terminal payments of the option:

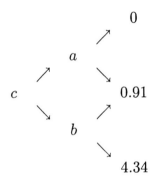

Year 0   Year 1   Year 2

The symbols a and b represent the unknown option values at year 1. By requiring that the option have expected one-period returns equal to the 1 year interest rate we can solve for these values:

$$1.12 = \frac{0.5(0 + 0.91)}{a}$$

$$a = \frac{0.5(0 + 0.91)}{1.12}$$

$$= 0.406$$

$$b = \frac{0.5(0.91 + 4.34)}{1.08}$$

$$= 2.43$$

We then use these values to work backwards and find c the value of the option today:

$$c = \frac{0.5(0.406 + 2.43)}{1.10}$$

$$= \$1.29$$

5.5.2   The n-period binomial model of Ho and Lee

We start our study of the n-period binomial tree by setting up a labelling system for the tree. Time is measured in integers starting at 0 and increasing by one at each set of new nodes. The possible states at each time are also denoted by an integer as follows:

```
                                    4
                          3
                 2               2
        1               1
0               0               0
       -1              -1
               -2              -2
                      -3
                              -4

0      1       2       3       4
```

Thus a particular node, say the highest node at time 2 is referred to as the node (2,2), and the lowest node at time 2 is denoted (2,-2).

In the Ho and Lee model interest rates change in a simple additive fashion. For example letting t measure time in quarters we can construct a quarterly Ho-Lee style tree by letting rates change in the following way:

$$r_{t+1} = r_t + \tfrac{1}{4}m_t \pm \sqrt{\tfrac{1}{4}} \text{ Vol (percentage points)}$$

We start with today's quarterly interest rate, say 5% and then calculate future rates by iterating on the above formula. For example if we choose a volatility of 1% and a drift m of zero our tree will start like this

$$
\begin{array}{ccccc}
 & & & & 6.5 \\
 & & & 6.0 & \\
 & & 5.5 & & 5.5 \\
 & 5.0 & & 5.0 & \\
 & & 4.5 & & 4.5 \\
 & & & 4.0 & \\
 & & & & 3.5 \\
\end{array}
$$

Note that the tree *recombines*. That is if we go down then up we end at the same spot as if we went up then down. A tree like this is easily constructed on a spreadsheet by simply copying and pasting one cell containing the up formula and another containing the down formula. Now let's assume that there is a risk-neutral probability of going up or down of exactly 0.5 at each branch of the tree. Surprisingly the information just given fully specifies a complete set of arbitrage-free prices for all zero-coupon bonds, for coupon bonds and for interest rate derivatives! As these model prices will, no doubt bear little resemblance to reality we shall need to alter the tree. But for now we shall see how the initial specification results in prices for bonds.

The principle of backward induction allows us to value any security by working backwards through the tree. Since all securities have expected return equal to the one-period riskless return, this implies that the value of a security today equals the expected discounted value of the security in the next period. Assuming simple interest rates this gives for a security

$$
V^i(0,0) = \frac{0.5(V^i(1,1) + V^i(1,-1))}{1 + r(0,0)/4}
$$

Similarly at say the up node in the next period we have

$$
V^i(1,1) = \frac{0.5(V^i(2,2) + V^i(2,0))}{1 + r(1,1)/4}
$$

and in the down node

$$
V^i(1,-1) = \frac{0.5(V^i(2,0) + V^i(2,-2))}{1 + r(1,-1)/4}
$$

The general formula is

$$V^i(t,j) = \frac{0.5(V^i(t+1,j+1) + V^i(t+1,j-1))}{1 + r(t,j)/4} \qquad (5.1)$$

We in fact start from the terminal payments of the security and then work backwards through the tree until we arrive at a value today.

For example a zero-coupon bond makes payments of its principal in each state at the maturity date. We can then discount these back one period to get a value at all states in the preceding time period. We continue on until we get back to a price today. This is extremely simple to program into a spreadsheet. Once the interest rate tree is constructed all securities can be valued.

5.5.3   The money-market account and the backward valuation formula

There is a particularly simple way of writing the backward valuation formula that relies on the concept of a *money-market account*. The value of this account is denoted $\mathcal{M}(t,i)$ at date t state i, or simply as $\mathcal{M}(t)$ when we do not wish to specify a particular state. The account starts off with value of one $\mathcal{M}(0,0) = 1$, and then grows by continually reinvesting at the one-period interest rate. Thus

$$\mathcal{M}(1,1) = 1 + r_0/4$$

for a quarterly tree, and

$$\mathcal{M}(T) = \prod_{i=0}^{T-1}(1 + r_i/4)$$

where the actual value of the money-market account will depend on the path of interest rates. Having established the money-market account we can now write the value of a random cash flow C_T as

$$V_0 = E\left[\frac{C_T}{\mathcal{M}(T)}\right]$$

where $E[.]$ is the expectation under risk-neutral probabilities. This expression can be derived by iterating backwards on the general one-period formula in (5.1).

A fundamental application of this formula is the pricing of a discount bond whose terminal payment C_T equals one:

$$B(0,T) = E\left[\frac{1}{\mathcal{M}(T)}\right]$$

5.6   Questions

1.1 Given the following interest rate tree for 1 year rates (equal risk-neutral probabilities)

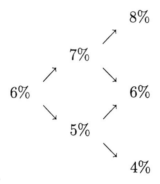

Year 0   Year 1   Year 2

value the 1, 2, and 3 year discount bonds, via backward induction.

1. Calculate the annual forward rate for a loan starting in year 2 and ending in year 3.

2. Does it equal the expected 1 year rate in year 2?

Chapter 6

State prices, forward induction, and tree-fitting

Although backward valuation provides an efficient method for valuing bonds and interest rate derivatives once a model and tree have been constructed, we have not yet examined how we choose the parameters that determine the interest rate tree. This process is called *fitting the tree*, and it is obviously very important. As a starting point we want our tree to correctly price all the actively traded securities that we have prices for. To do so we proceed in several steps. We first choose an interest rate process, and construct a tree with arbitrary parameters. From this we use the principle of *forward induction* to construct a set of state prices. From these state prices we construct model prices for the securities we have market prices for. Next we alter the parameters of the interest rate process so as to minimize the divergence between model and market prices.

We first review state prices in a multi-period context and then show how forward induction can be used to provide a set of state prices.

6.1 State prices and valuation

Recall from the one-period example in Chapter 5 that a state price is the price of a fictitious security paying one dollar in a particular state and zero in other states. In a multi-period setting we label a state price by $G(t, j, T, k)$, where the first two arguments refer to the current node, i.e. time t and state j, and the next two arguments refer to the node for which the payment of $1 is promised, i.e. time T and state k. Often we shall be concerned with state prices for time 0 which have the simpler label $G(0, 0, T, k)$. The reason that we are interested in state prices is that they provide a very simple valuation formula — even simpler than the backward induction valuation formula. Consider a random cash flow at time T which we label

$$X_T = (X(T, k), X(T, k - 2), \ldots, X(T, -k + 2), X(T, -k))$$

this notation simply shows the payments in each of the states at date T. To find the value of this cash flow at time 0, we could use backward induction to arrive at a value today. Alternatively, if we had a set of state prices for each of the states at date T we could use the principle of value additivity and value the cash flow by simply multiplying each state-contingent cash flow by its state price and summing across all possible states:

$$V(X_T) = \sum_{i \in \{k, k-2, \ldots, -k\}} G(0, 0, T, i) X(T, i)$$

Valuation is thus a simple process involving multiplication and addition. In order to be able to use this formula we need to be able to calculate the state prices implied by a particular tree, and this is the subject of the next section.

6.2   Forward induction and the state-price tree

In order to construct a tree of state prices we use a principle called *forward induction*. This principle is also known as the Fokker–Planck equation or the forward Kolmogorov equation. Despite the daunting titles we shall see that this equation is easily understood in terms of the (by now) familiar triangular arbitrage relations (Figure 6.1).

Our aim is to construct a complete set of state prices for the current date, given some interest rate tree. Thus we are trying to find state prices $G(0, 0, T, j)$ for all future dates T and for all states j. We start at the beginning of the tree. Since a dollar today has value of one dollar we have

$$G(0, 0, 0, 0) = 1$$

The next two nodes have state prices labelled $G(0, 0, 1, 1)$ and $G(0, 0, 1, -1)$. These prices are found by using the principle of risk-neutral pricing. A security paying one dollar in the up node must have an expected return equal to

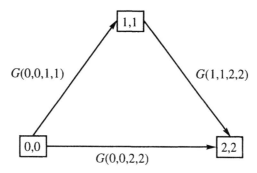

Figure 6.1 State price relationships

the interest rate. We thus have that

$$\frac{\frac{1}{2} \cdot 1 + \frac{1}{2} \cdot 0}{G(0,0,1,1)} = 1 + r(0,0)\Delta$$

so that

$$G(0,0,1,1) = \frac{1/2}{1 + r(0,0)\Delta}$$

$$G(0,0,1,-1) = \frac{1/2}{1 + r(0,0)\Delta}$$

Consider a security paying \$1 at the node $(2, 2)$. An alternative way to achieve this cash flow would be to buy the A–D security paying at $(1, 1)$ and then buy at node $(1, 1)$ the A–D security paying at $(2, 2)$. These two alternative strategies can be shown in a triangle diagram (Figure 6.2).

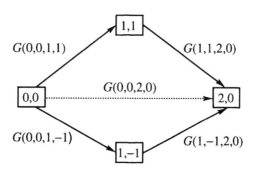

Figure 6.2 The forward equation

The usual triangular arbitrage requirement then implies that

$$G(0,0,2,2) = G(0,0,1,1) \times G(1,1,2,2)$$

Now the state price $G(1,1,2,2)$ is given from the principle of risk-neutral valuation in the same way as $G(0,0,1,1)$. Thus we have that

$$G(1,1,2,2) = \frac{1/2}{1 + r(1,1)\Delta}$$

resulting in the following expression:

$$G(0,0,2,2) = G(0,0,1,1) \times \frac{1/2}{1 + r(1,1)\Delta}$$

We can continue out along the upper and lower limbs of the tree using this formula to get state prices further out in time. For nodes not on the upper or lower limbs we need to alter the expression somewhat.

Consider the state price of the A–D security paying a dollar at node (2, 0). Since there are two ways that this node can be arrived at — up–down and down–up, we need to buy two securities. Again a diagram should make this clear. In order to achieve a cash flow of $1 at node (2, 0) using indirect means we need to purchase both the upper strategy *and* the lower strategy. The no-arbitrage pricing restriction is that

$$G(0,0,2,0) = G(0,0,1,1) \times G(1,1,2,0)$$
$$+ G(0,0,1,-1) \times G(1,-1,2,0)$$

This can be expressed as

$$G(0,0,2,2) = G(0,0,1,1) \times \frac{1/2}{1 + r(1,1)\Delta}$$

$$+ G(0,0,1,-1) \times \frac{1/2}{1 + r(1,-1)\Delta}$$

We can write this expression in general terms as

$$G(0,0,t,j) = \frac{0.5 \times G(0,0,t-1,j+1)}{1 + r(t-1,j+1)\Delta} + \frac{0.5 \times G(0,0,t-1,j-1)}{1 + r(t-1,j-1)\Delta}$$

With this formula and an interest rate tree, we can sweep forward filling in state prices to create a whole tree of state prices.

Let's use this method to construct a state price tree for the annual interest rate tree used in Chapter 5, which we repeat here.

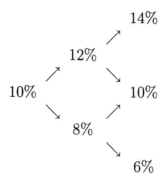

Year 0   Year 1   Year 2

We know the first state price is simply one so we can include that in a state price tree:

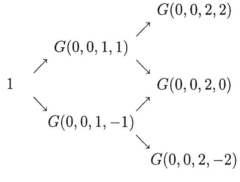

Year 0   Year 1   Year 2

Now if we purchase at time 0 the state claim paying $1 in $(1, 1)$ for a price of $G(0, 0, 1, 1)$ the expected return from this security is

$$\frac{0.5 \cdot 1 + 0.5 \cdot 0}{G(0, 0, 1, 1)}$$

Since these probabilities are risk-neutral probabilities this expected return must equal the riskless return:

$$\frac{0.5}{G(0, 0, 1, 1)} = 1.10$$

$$G(0, 0, 1, 1) = \frac{0.5}{1.1}$$

$$= 0.455$$

The same logic applies to the state claim paying off in $(1,-1)$:

$$G(0,0,1,-1) = \frac{0.5}{1.1}$$
$$= 0.455$$

Thus we can fill in year 1 of the state tree with these prices:

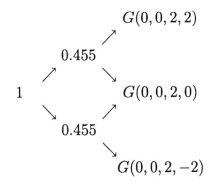

$$
\begin{array}{c}
 \hspace{3cm} G(0,0,2,2) \\[-2pt]
\hspace{3cm} \nearrow \\[-2pt]
0.455 \\[-2pt]
\nearrow \hspace{1.2cm} \searrow \\[-2pt]
1 \hspace{2cm} G(0,0,2,0) \\[-2pt]
\searrow \hspace{1.2cm} \nearrow \\[-2pt]
0.455 \\[-2pt]
\searrow \\[-2pt]
\hspace{3cm} G(0,0,2,-2)
\end{array}
$$

Year 0   Year 1   Year 2

Using the forward induction equation in (6.1) we can find the remaining values as

$$G(0,0,2,2) = 0 + \frac{0.5 \times 0.455}{1.12}$$
$$= 0.203$$

and

$$G(0,0,2,0) = \frac{0.5 \times 0.455}{1.12} + \frac{0.5 \times 0.455}{1.08}$$
$$= 0.414$$

and

$$G(0,0,2,-2) = \frac{0.5 \times 0.455}{1.08} + 0$$
$$= 0.212$$

The completed state price tree:

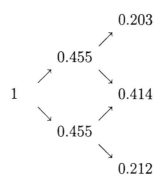

Year 0   Year 1   Year 2

can now be used to price securities. Consider the bond option which made payments in year 2 of $(0, 0.91, 4.34)$. Using the state prices at year 2 we can value this option by

$$V = 0.203 \times 0 + 0.414 \times 0.91 + 0.212 \times 4.34$$

$$= \$1.29$$

which is the same valuation as that obtained using backward induction in Chapter 5.

6.3   Interest rate trees

The first thing to be decided is the interest rate model that will be used. Different models imply different types of behaviour of interest rates. For example the simplest model is a Ho–Lee model in which the interest rate at a particular point on the tree evolves with constant absolute volatility. Thus the general form for an up-branch from a node is given by:

$$r(i + 1, j + 1) = r(i, j) + \Delta m_i + \sqrt{\Delta}\sigma, \quad \text{with probability } 1/2$$

and the general form for a down-branch is

$$r(i + 1, j + 1) = r(i, j) + \Delta m_i - \sqrt{\Delta}\sigma \quad \text{with probability } 1/2$$

In these equations Δ refers to the time interval of steps in the tree expressed as fractions of a year. The *drift* in the short rate is the symbol m_i, where the subscript i means that this drift can vary from period to period, though it remains the same for all states in a given period. The drift is expressed in annual terms so that a drift of 0.01 implies that the short rate is expected (under the risk-neutral probabilities) to increase over the next interval at a rate of 1 percentage point per year.

The term σ is the volatility expressed in absolute annual terms. It is multiplied by $\sqrt{\Delta}$ in order to scale the price change in the appropriate way to allow for the fact that the interval will not in general equal one year.

The interval must be chosen and will depend in part on the type of instruments being valued. Often a tree with quarterly steps will suffice. The dates can then be chosen to coincide with T-bill or Eurodollar futures maturities.

6.3.1 Technical note

One obvious problem that arises is that, in general the current date will not be exactly one quarter from the next futures maturity date. The question then arises as to how to construct the initial step in the tree. The aim is to produce a process which in this first step has drift and volatility over the interval that produces the required annual drift and volatility, but also results in interest rates next period that will recombine.

The procedure we suggest is as follows. Say the current date is one month from the next futures maturity date, and that we are using a quarterly rate tree. The following time step is then in 4 months (3 months + 1 month) time. At this point in time three rates are chosen given by

$$r(4 \text{ months}, 1) = r(0,0) + \frac{4}{12}m_0 + 2\sqrt{\frac{3}{12}}\sigma$$

$$r(4 \text{ months}, 0) = r(0,0) + \frac{4}{12}m_0$$

$$r(4 \text{ months}, -1) = r(0,0) + \frac{4}{12}m_0 - 2\sqrt{\frac{3}{12}}\sigma$$

Note that the drift is multiplied by $4/12$ but the volatility must be multiplied by $\sqrt{3/12}$, so that all rates will be spaced equally apart so that they will recombine.

Now the trick is that the probabilities for this trinomial branching process need to be chosen so that the drift is correct and the variance is equal to

$$\frac{4}{12}\sigma^2$$

The drift will be matched by setting the up and down probabilities equal. Call this probability p, then the middle probability must be $1 - 2p$, since probabilities must sum to one. The variance is then given by

$$2p2^2 \frac{3}{12}\sigma^2 = 2p\sigma^2$$

Setting this equal to the required variance of $4\sigma^2/12$ then gives the appropriate probability p of

$$p = \frac{1}{6}$$

With the initial step accounted for in this way, an interest rate tree can be constructed. This is easily done in a spreadsheet package by copying and pasting cells for up-branches and for down-branches. Note that the probability is not required for construction of an interest rate tree. The probability is important in the calculation of state prices.

For the case in which the current time is not an exact step from the next futures termination date, the prices at the three nodes in the first step are given by

$$G(0,0,2,2) = \frac{p}{1 + r(0,0)h}$$

$$G(0,0,2,0) = \frac{1 - 2p}{1 + r(0,0)h}$$

$$G(0,0,2,-2) = \frac{p}{1 + r(0,0)h}$$

where p is the probability as worked out before and h is the length of time (in years) to the second futures maturity date.

6.4 Fitting market prices

With an interest rate and a state-price tree constructed the fitting of the model to market prices is actually quite straightforward. The first step is to calculate model prices. For the case of the Ho–Lee model, we fit bond prices. The simplest method is to calculate a set of zero-coupon bond prices and fit these. Model zero-coupon bond prices are simply given as the sum of a set of zero-coupon bond prices for a given date. That is

$$B(0,T) = \sum_i G(0,0,T,i)$$

The starting interest rate $r(0,0)$ can simply be chosen to fit the short bill price. From then on the parameter that controls the general level of interest rates is the drift parameter m.

The basic procedure is to adjust m in each time period so as to minimize the squared difference between model and market prices.

6.5   Questions

1. Given the following rate tree, calculate a state price tree.

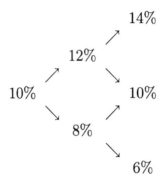

Year 0   Year 1   Year 2

1. Value a caplet with expiration in year 2, strike of 9.5% and reference rate the annual rate.

Chapter 7

The Black–Derman–Toy model

The Black–Derman–Toy model (hereafter BDT) has become an industry standard for single factor interest rate models. The reason is twofold. First, unlike the Ho–Lee model it guarantees that interest rates remain non-negative. Second, it can be used to fit a term structure of volatilities as well as a term structure of rates. Implementation of the BDT model is typically via a binomial tree. Before examining the implementation of the model we first look at the model characteristics.

7.1   Model characteristics

The BDT model is characterized by the fact that the short-term default-free rate of interest is distributed lognormally. This means that the log of the interest rate is itself normally distributed. This has two benefits. First it results in the interest rate always being positive. There is zero probability that the rate will become negative. Second it leads to a natural description of volatility as a proportional volatility rather than an absolute volatility. The market uses proportional measures of volatility, so the BDT model matches market conventions in this respect.

Not all models use proportional volatility. For example the Ho–Lee model uses absolute rather than proportional volatility. An example is the clearest way of illustrating the difference between the two concepts. Assume the 1 year rate is currently 10% and that in 1 year's time it will either rise to 11% or fall to 9% with equal probability. The absolute volatility is given as

$$\text{Abs. Vol} = \tfrac{1}{2}(11 - 9)$$
$$= 1\% \text{ p.a.}$$

The proportional volatility is calculated using logs:

$$\text{Prop. Vol} = \frac{1}{2}(\ln 11 - \ln 9)$$

$$= \frac{1}{2}\ln\frac{11}{9}$$

$$= 10.03\% \text{ p.a.}$$

Note that the proportional volatility calculated using logs is approximately equal to the absolute volatility divided by the absolute level of rates:

$$\text{Prop. Vol} \approx \frac{\text{Abs. Vol}}{10\%}$$

$$\approx \frac{1\%}{10\%} = 10\%$$

7.2   Implementing BDT

It turns out that a variable will be lognormally distributed at all points in time, if for any particular point in time, the proportional one-step volatility is constant across all states. However the one-step volatility can differ across dates. Let's assume that we have a term structure of one-step volatilities given to us (perhaps reflecting trader's views). We also have a complete set of discount bonds prices. The problem then is to construct a tree of interest rates that fits both the term structure of spot rates and the term structure of volatilities. Although this may sound complex it is in fact very simple to do. We label the nodes of the tree in the usual way starting from (0,0). At each date $1, 2, \ldots$ we label the one-step volatility as $v_1, v_2, \ldots$. We then construct the tree in the following way:

c	c_0	c_1	c_2	c_3
v		v_1	v_2	v_3
3				$\exp(c_3 + 3 \cdot v_3)$
2			$\exp(c_2 + 2 \cdot v_2)$	
1		$\exp(c_1 + 1 \cdot v_1)$		$\exp(c_3 + 1 \cdot v_3)$
0	$\exp(c_0)$		$\exp(c_2 + 0 \cdot v_2)$	
−1		$\exp(c_1 - 1 \cdot v_1)$		$\exp(c_3 - 1 \cdot v_3)$
−2			$\exp(c_2 - 2 \cdot v_2)$	
−3				$\exp(c_3 - 3 \cdot v_3)$
	0	1	2	3

The parameter c_t controls the central rate at date t the parameter v_t controls the one-step volatility at t. Assuming that we have been given a set of volatilities v, we only need to solve for the central rates c. To do this we use these rates to construct a tree of state prices just as in the Ho–Lee case by using the principle of forward induction. With a state price tree model zero prices can be calculated simply by summing the state prices in a particular column to give the price of the zero maturing at that date. We then use an optimizing routine such as Solver in Excel to minimize the sum of squared deviations between model and market prices, letting the central rates $c_0, c_1, \ldots$ change. If we had information on the market prices of instruments sensitive to volatility such as interest rate floors and caps, we could also solve for the volatilities $v_1, v_2, \ldots$ that would correctly price these instruments.

7.3   Example: the bias in Eurodollar futures

What can one do with an interest rate tree? One of the most useful things we can do is formally examine the mark-to-market or *resettlement* feature of futures contracts that, until now, we have ignored. Consider a quarterly tree constructed for the Eurodollar LIBOR market. We take the tree as given, and ask, 'what is the price of a 3 month Eurodollar futures contract, taking account of the resettlement feature of futures?'

For modelling purposes, we can describe resettlement as follows. We take as given some (as yet unknown) process for futures prices, that we could place on a tree, e.g. $f(0,0)$ today, $f(1,1)$ and $f(1,-1)$ next period, and so on. Now an investor who purchases one futures contract is agreeing to accept the resettlement payment $f(t+1,.) - f(t,.)$ at time $t+1$, the payment $f(t+2,.) - f(t+1,.)$ at time $t+2$ and so on, until the position is eliminated or the contract expires at time T. At expiration, we have the simple boundary condition that $100 - f(T,j) = L(T,j)$, where $L(T,j)$ is the 3 month LIBOR rate prevailing at expiration at node T.

To calculate the futures price process, we work backwards through the tree, using the principle of backward induction. However there is a slight twist to the backward valuation formula—there is *no discounting*! At any node the futures price is simply the expectation of the futures price at the following two nodes.

To see this, consider the 'purchase' of a futures contract at (t,j) and the disposal of the contract at $(t+1, j \pm 1)$. At the two nodes $(t+1, j \pm 1)$ we receive the amount $f(t+1, j \pm 1) - f(t,j)$. Since this payment is costless, it has zero value, and under risk-neutral probabilities, it must have an expected value of zero:

$$E[f(t+1, j \pm 1) - f(t, j)] = 0,$$
$$f(t, j) = E[f(t+1, j \pm 1)]$$

Thus futures prices are given by working back from the expiration date, with the futures price at (t, j) being given as the average of futures prices in the following two nodes. Iterating backwards on this formula we have the result that the futures price today is simply the expectation of the futures price at maturity:

$$f(0, 0) = E[f(T, .)]$$

How does this price compare with the forward rate implied by the term structure? This question can be answered by construction of a tree. Alternatively, we can derive an expression for the forward rate that illuminates the difference between futures and forward rates.

We denote the forward rate as of today between T and $T + \frac{1}{4}$ as $F(0, T, T + 1/4)$. This forward rate is given by

$$F(0, T, T + 1/4) = 4 \times \left(\frac{B(0, T)}{B(0, T + 1/4)} - 1 \right)$$

Noting that under risk-neutral expectations the discount bond price is given in terms of the money-market account by $B(0, T) = E[\mathcal{M}(T)^{-1}]$, and that $\mathcal{M}(T + 1/4) = \mathcal{M}(T)(1 + r_T/4)$ we can write the forward rate as

$$F(0, T, T + 1/4) = 4 \times \left(\frac{E[\mathcal{M}(T)^{-1}]}{E[(\mathcal{M}(T)(1 + r_T/4))^{-1}]} - 1 \right)$$

$$= \frac{4}{B(0, T + 1/4)} \times [E[\mathcal{M}(T)^{-1}] - E(\mathcal{M}(T)(1 + r_T/4))^{-1}]$$

$$= \frac{4}{B(0, T + 1/4)} \times E\left[\mathcal{M}(T)^{-1} \left(1 - \frac{1}{1 + r_T/4} \right) \right]$$

$$= \frac{4}{B(0, T + 1/4)} \times E\left[\mathcal{M}(T)^{-1} \left(\frac{r_T/4}{1 + r_T/4} \right) \right]$$

$$= \frac{4}{B(0, T + 1/4)} \times E\left[\mathcal{M}(T + 1/4)^{-1} r_T/4 \right]$$

In other words the forward rate is an average over the possible rates (r_{4T}) that will prevail between T and $T + 1/4$. The weights that are used in this average are the risk-neutral probabilities as well as the money-market account. The difference from the futures rate is the fact that the money-market account is a weighting factor. The result is that for forward rates more weight is given to low interest rates (since low interest rates are associated with high $\mathcal{M}(T + 1/4)^{-1}$, so that the forward rate will be below the rate implied from futures prices.

7.4 Example: valuation of an interest rate caplet

Consider a European caplet which pays an amount $\max(L(T, T + 1/4) - K, 0)$ at the expiration date T. To value this we construct a tree, either quarterly or finer such as weekly, and simply calculate the payment $\max(L(T, T + 1/4) - K, 0)$ at each node at T. Value can then be found by multiplying these payments by state prices and adding, or by backward induction.

7.5 Example: valuation of a general FRN

We consider the valuation of a single random cashflow from a general FRN. The complete FRN can then be valued by applying the same method to each cashflow in turn and summing the resultant values. Say the payment occurs at T and it is stipulated to equal the prevailing yield on a 3 year discount bond. Valuation proceeds in two steps: (i) calculation of cash flows at each node at T; (ii) valuation of cash flows using state prices.

For step one we need to calculate the price of a 3 year zero at each node of T. This is most easily done using backward valuation. In a backward valuation tree insert ones at all nodes at year $T + 3$. The tree will then give us a set of prices at all preceding nodes. We focus on the prices at time T. These prices are then converted to yields using the stipulated convention. These yields are the cash flows that will be paid at date T. We can now move to step 2 — valuation by state prices — which is quite straightforward.

7.6   Further reading

1. Black, F. (1995) 'Interest Rates as Options', *The Journal of Finance*, 50(7).

2. Black, F., Derman, E. and Toy (1990) 'A One-Factor Model of Interest Rates and Its Application to Treasury Bond Options', *Financial Analysts Journal*.

3. Kirikos, G. and D. Novak (1997) 'Convexity Conundrums', *RISK*, 10(3).

7.7   Questions

1. Using US Treasury 'strip' prices from the WSJ, construct a quarterly BDT tree model with constant volatility of 10% p.a. that fits these prices.

2. Design an interest rate option, such as a caplet, or bond option and value it using the interest rate tree (plus a state price tree).

3. Redo the interest rate tree and option valuation assuming interest rate volatility is 20% p.a.

Chapter 8

Convexity

So far we have managed to avoid explicitly dealing with the fact that bond prices are nonlinear functions of discount rates. Figure 8.1 shows the price–(vertical axis) yield (horizontal axis) relationship for 10, 20, and 30 year zero-coupon bonds (annual compounding).

Of course all three lines are downward sloping (higher yields mean lower bond prices), but this slope is not constant. The line is curved with a bow downwards. A function with this shape is called convex, and this characteristic of bonds is known as convexity. Convexity is a surprisingly pervasive factor in the analysis of bonds and their derivatives. It was originally used to increase the accuracy of answers to the question, 'if yields move up a

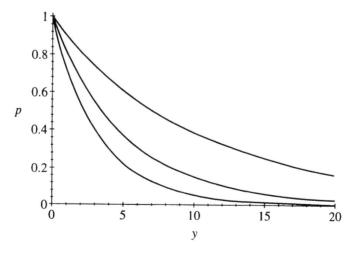

Figure 8.1 Price–yield relationship for zero-coupon bonds

percentage point, how much value will my portfolio lose?' More recently convexity has become important for the valuation of non-generic swaps and general floating rate notes. Finally convexity provides the explanation to why yield curves are often humped with long forward rates falling. Understanding convexity is thus important. We start with a brief introduction to the mathematics of curvature.

8.1 Curvature

Mathematically speaking, the curvature of a function is described by the second derivative of the function. Using a discrete approximation, we have that the first derivative is the *slope* of the function

$$\frac{df}{dx} \simeq \frac{\Delta f}{\Delta x}$$

and the second derivative is the *rate of change* of the slope

$$\frac{d^2 f}{dx^2} = \frac{\Delta \left(\frac{\Delta f}{\Delta x} \right)}{\Delta x}$$

The second derivative is calculated by differentiation of the first derivative. Thus if we have a function of x say

$$f(x) = x^4$$

then the first derivative is

$$f'(x) = 4x^3$$

and differentiating this expression gives the second derivative:

$$f''(x) = 12x^2$$

Note that a straight line function

$$f(x) = a + bx$$

has a second derivative of zero indicating that it has zero curvature:

$$f'(x) = b$$
$$f''(x) = 0$$

8.1.1   The Taylor series approximation

The major use we will make of second derivatives is in a Taylor series approximation, which is a very useful mathematical tool. The purpose of a Taylor series approximation is to approximate the behaviour of a function over some small range just by using the first and second derivatives of the function. For example say we are interested in the price behaviour of a 10 year discount bond in response to its spot rate, but particularly around the 10% level. The first-order Taylor series approximation is given by

$$f(x) \approx f(\overline{x}) + f'(\overline{x})(x - \overline{x})$$

where $\overline{x} \equiv 10\%$. Let's examine this function one term at a time. The first term $f(x)$ is the function that we are approximating. We want to know what the value of the function is when evaluated at x. The point is that we do not know what the value is for general x, however we do know what the value is when evaluated at $\overline{x}$. This value is given by the symbol $f(\overline{x})$. The symbol $\approx$ simply means approximately equal to rather than exactly equal to. The next term $f'(\overline{x})$ is the first derivative of the function. If this first derivative can change, i.e. the function is a curved or nonlinear one then it is important that we evaluate this first derivative at $\overline{x}$.

Now let's consider the 10 year zero-coupon bond price. We call the price p and the yield y. In this case we know the actual formula

$$p(y) = \frac{1}{(1 + y)^{10}}$$

The first-order Taylor series approximation to this formula is

$$p(y) = p(10\%) + p'(10\%)(y - 10\%)$$

We can evaluate the terms in this expression:

$$p(10\%) = 0.385\,54$$

$$p'(10\%) = -10 \times (1.1)^{-11}$$

$$= -3.505$$

Thus the first-order approximation to the function is

$$p(y) \approx 0.385\,54 - 3.505(y - 0.1)$$

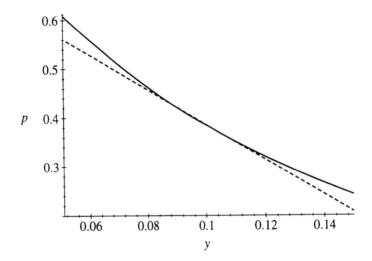

Figure 8.2 Actual price relationship *vs* Taylor series approximation

The solid line in Figure 8.2 shows the actual price–yield relationship and the dotted line shows the Taylor series approximation (around 10%) to the relationship.

The formula for a second-order Taylor series approximation takes the curvature of the function into account. The formula is

$$f(x) \approx f(\overline{x}) + f'(\overline{x})(x - \overline{x}) + \tfrac{1}{2}f''(\overline{x})(x - \overline{x})^2$$

where the squared term is designed to capture the curvature of the function.

The derivatives of the price–yield relationship are

$$p(y) = (1 + y)^{-10}$$
$$p'(y) = -10(1 + y)^{-11}$$
$$p''(y) = 110(1 + y)^{-12}$$

Evaluating the second derivative at 10% gives

$$p''(0.1) = 35.049$$

and the second-order Taylor series approximation is $35.049/2 = 17.525$

$$p(y) \approx 0.385\,54 - 3.505(y - 0.1) + 17.525(y - 0.1)^2$$

Figure 8.3 shows that this second-order expansion, shown as the dotted line, is more accurate over a larger range of values.

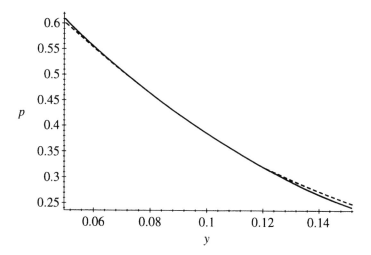

Figure 8.3 Second order expansion

8.1.2   Bond convexity

You will recall that modified duration was defined as the first derivative of the price–yield relationship scaled by the price:

$$\text{Modified duration} = \frac{1}{P}\frac{dP}{dy}$$

Bond curvature is described in an analogous way by convexity which is the second derivative scaled by price:

$$\text{Convexity} = \frac{1}{P}\frac{d^2P}{dy^2}$$

You will also recall that duration was defined as the value-average time to payments. For convexity the analogous definition is as the value-average *squared time* to payments. This is easily seen using continuous compounding and a zero-coupon bond. We have the following relationships for a zero maturing in T years:

$$P(y) = \exp(-yT)$$

$$P'(y) = -T\exp(-yT)$$

$$\text{Duration} = \frac{1}{P}P'(y) = -T$$

$$P''(y) = T^2 \exp(-yT)$$

$$\text{Convexity} = \frac{1}{P}P''(y) = T^2$$

Using annual compounding we can calculate modified duration and convexity in the following way for a zero-coupon bond.

$$P(y) = (1+y)^{-T}$$

$$P'(y) = -T(1+y)^{-T-1}$$

$$\text{Mod. duration} = \frac{1}{P}P'(y) = \frac{-T}{(1+y)}$$

$$P''(y) = T(T+1)(1+y)^{-T-2}$$

$$\text{Convexity} = \frac{1}{P}P''(y) = \frac{T(T+1)}{(1+y)^2}$$

The result is that if we know the duration *and* the convexity of a bond, we can get a more accurate answer to the question, 'how much value is lost if the yield rises by a certain amount?' The formula is as follows

$$\text{New price} = \text{Old price} - \left[\frac{\text{Old price}}{100} \times D_{\text{mod}} \times \Delta y\right]$$

$$+ \frac{1}{2}\left[\frac{\text{Old price}}{100} \times \text{Convexity} \times (\Delta y)^2\right]$$

where D_{mod} is modified duration, and Δy is the change in yield in percentage point (e.g. if yields rise from 7% to 8% then $\Delta y = 1$). Of course an even more accurate answer can be obtained via evaluation of the pricing formula, and with modern calculators this is very easy. However convexity is important for other reasons.

8.1.3 Jensen's inequality

One of the reasons convexity is important, results from a mathematical fact known as Jensen's inequality. This inequality says that for a convex function $f(x)$ the expectation of the function is always greater than the function of the expectation. It is perhaps more clearly expressed in mathematical notation:

$$E[f(x)] \geq f(E[x])$$

Let's take the simplest example I can think of. A simple convex function is $f(x) = x^2$. Now let's assume that x has a binomial distribution with equally likely outcomes of 0 and 2. We can now check Jensen's inequality

$$E[f(x)] = 0.5 \times (x = 0)^2 + 0.5 \times (x = 2)^2$$
$$= 2$$

and the right-hand side of the inequality is given by

$$f(E[x]) = f(1)$$
$$= 1$$

So the inequality held for this case. Another way of understanding the inequality more generally is via a second-order Taylor series approximation. We label $E[x]$ by $\bar{x}$, and we then take the expectation of the Taylor series approximation:

$$E[f(x)] \approx E\left[f(\bar{x}) + f'(\bar{x})(x - \bar{x}) + \tfrac{1}{2}f''(\bar{x})(x - \bar{x})^2\right]$$

Now the expressions $f(\bar{x})$, $f'(\bar{x})$, and $f''(\bar{x})$ are known and non-random, hence we can take them out of the expectation giving

$$E[f(x)] \approx f(\bar{x}) + f'(\bar{x})E[x - \bar{x}] + \tfrac{1}{2}f''(\bar{x})E[(x - \bar{x})^2]$$

Since $E[x - \bar{x}] = 0$, the second term drops out leaving us with

$$E[f(x)] \approx f(\bar{x}) + \tfrac{1}{2}f''(\bar{x})E[(x - \bar{x})^2]$$

Now it is a mathematical fact that all convex functions have positive second derivatives. Thus f'' is positive, and of course the term $E[(x - \bar{x})^2]$ is positive so we have that the second term is positive implying that (at least approximately)

$$E[f(x)] \geq f(\bar{x})$$

In fact the Taylor series approximation can help in telling us how great the inequality is. The term $E[(x - \bar{x})^2]$ is the variance of x, so we have that the greater the variance and the greater the curvature or second derivative the greater the inequality.

8.2   The convexity adjustment for swap and FRN valuation

We have seen that interest rate swaps can typically be broken down into two components, a fixed leg which is like a fixed coupon bond, and a floating leg which is like a floating rate note. The types of swaps we analysed previously were simple swaps meaning that the floating leg was a *perfect* floating rate note. Recall that a perfect floating rate note is always valued at par at reset dates because the reset date of the next coupon coincides with the current coupon payment date and the base rate which determines the floating payment is equal to the period rate (i.e. quarterly payments tied to 3 month Libor). For the simple interest rate swap valuation was quite simple once a set of spot rates was found for valuing the fixed side.

More general interest rate swaps have floating legs that can be viewed as *general* floating rate notes. The tricky part of valuing such swaps then boils down to valuing the general floating rate note, and this is more difficult as it need not be valued at par at reset dates.

An example of a general floating rate note would be a bond making semi-annual floating payments equal to half the prevailing yield on a 5 year Treasury bond. There is no simple strategy that can replicate this payment so one approach is to use an interest rate tree to value such a security. For each coupon payment date we can calculate the yield on a 5 year bond at each node. From this we calculate the payment at each node and we can then value the floating coupon either via backward induction or by using state prices (multiply and add).

However there is an alternative model-free approximate way of pricing such floating payments. The method is based on forward rates and a convexity adjustment, but first we shall need to understand a little of a very recent approach to derivative valuation which involves changing probabilities.

8.2.1   Changes of probability

We saw previously that the absence of arbitrage guaranteed the existence of a set of state prices. From these state prices we were able to infer a set of risk-neutral probabilities, that could be used for pricing all securities.

You may recall that state prices had two of the defining characteristics of probabilities: positivity and additivity. But the set of state prices does not sum to one. We therefore had to adjust state prices so that they would sum to one. The result was as if we were in an economy that was risk-neutral over one period. All assets had expected return over one period that was equal to the one-period riskless rate.

Now surprisingly, this does not imply that all assets will have the same expected return over two periods.

For example consider the following binomial tree in 1 year short rates. The (one-period) risk-neutral probabilities of up and down moves are equal.

$$
\begin{array}{ccc}
 & & 25 \\
 & 20 & \\
10 & & 10 \\
 & 5 & \\
 & & 3
\end{array}
$$

The first 2 years of the state price tree implied by this rate tree is as follows:

$$
\begin{array}{ccc}
 & & 0.1894 \\
 & 0.454 & \\
1 & & 0.40585 \\
 & 0.454 & \\
 & & 0.2164
\end{array}
$$

Now let's examine the price processes for the state claims paying off at date 2. The prices are calculated using backward induction, i.e. expected returns at each point in time must equal the prevailing period rate. Applying these principles results in the following three price processes:

$$
\begin{array}{ccc}
 & 1 & \\
0.41667 & & 0 \\
0.1894 & & 0 & 0.40585 \\
 & 0 & \\
 & & 0
\end{array}
\qquad
\begin{array}{ccc}
 & 0 & \\
0.41667 & & 0 \\
1 & 0.21645 & 0.47619 \\
 & 0 & \\
\end{array}
\qquad
\begin{array}{ccc}
 & 0 & \\
 & 0 & \\
 & & 0 \\
 & 0.47619 & \\
 & & 1
\end{array}
$$

Now it is easy to check that each of these securities has an expected one-period return equal to the prevailing one-period riskless rate. The expected

2 year returns are in order

$$\frac{0.25 \cdot 1}{0.1894} - 1 = 31.996\%$$

for the first security,

$$\frac{0.5 \cdot 1}{0.40585} - 1 = 23.198\%$$

for the second security and

$$\frac{0.25 \cdot 1}{0.21645} - 1 = 15.5\%$$

for the third security.

Although all securities have equal one-period expected returns the expected returns over two periods are quite different. This is annoying when we wish to value a payment occurring at a particular date that is more than one period away. It would be nice to have a set of probabilities such that all securities would earn the same return over the period until this payment date. Of course it would be nicer still to have a set of probabilities such that all securities earned the same return over all dates, but this is impossible when interest rates are stochastic.

However, it is easy to construct probabilities such that all payments at a particular date have the same expected return. This date is generally referred to as date T and the probability is called the T-measure.

We construct the T-measure in the following way. Simply divide the state prices for events at date T by the price of the zero-coupon bond maturing at date T. In other words divide by the sum of the state prices. In the above case this gives T-measure probabilities of

$$\frac{0.189}{0.189 + 0.406 + 0.216}, \quad \frac{0.406}{0.811}, \quad \text{and} \quad \frac{0.2164}{0.811}$$

Using these probabilities all securities making payments solely at date 2 will have the same expected return.

In general if we have state prices at all states j for a particular date T, then by defining the T-measure by

$$\pi(j) = \frac{G(0,0,T,j)}{\sum_{j} G(0,0,T,j)} = \frac{G(0,0,T,j)}{B(0,T)}$$

we can form the valuation formula for a random cash flow c_T at T by the discounted value of the expected cash flow:

$$V_0 = B(0,T)E^T[c_T]$$

To prove this result we start from the general valuation formula:

$$V_0 = \sum_j G(0,0,T,j)c(T,j)$$

Now divide and multiply by the zero price (which equals the sum of state prices):

$$V_0 = B(0,T)\sum_j \frac{G(0,0,T,j)}{B(0,T)}c(T,j)$$

$$= B(0,T)\sum_j \pi(j)c(T,j)$$

$$= B(0,T)E^T[c_T]$$

Now recall the risk-neutral backward valuation formula

$$V_0 = E[\mathcal{M}(T)^{-1}C_T]$$

and note the difference. Discounting is done by the reciprocal of the money-market account and this is random, whereas under the T-measure, discounting is done by a known quantity — the price of the discount bond. We now use the T-measure to derive an alternative way of valuing a perfect FRN and a simple interest rate swap. We then examine an approximate method for valuing general FRNs.

8.2.2   Forward rates and perfect FRNs

Consider a single payment of a perfect FRN. The payment at T can generally be written as the Libor rate prevailing at the reset date multiplied by the time between payments

$$L(T-h,T) \times h = \frac{1}{B(T-h,T)} - 1$$

where h is the time between coupon payments. We can value this by replication. Today we buy a zero maturing at $T - h$ and we sell a zero maturing at T. At $T - h$ when the first zero matures we rollover into the h-period zero. At T we then receive the sum $1/B(T - h, T)$ and we repay the short position in the second zero, producing the cash flow as above. Thus the cost of this strategy is equal to

$$B(0, T - h) - B(0, T)$$

and this must be the value of the random payment. Now let's for the moment assume we know the T-measure and that we can use these probabilities for calculating expectations. An expectation under the T-measure is denoted $E^T[.]$. Under this expectation all securities earn the same expected return over the period 0 to T. Any payment c_T at date T can then be valued simply by using the T-measure valuation formula:

$$V_0 = B(0, T) E^T[c_T]$$

This formula simply follows from the fact that under the T-measure all securities earn the same expected return over the interval from now to T. We can use this formula to value the floating coupon. The formula is simple:

$$V_0 = B(0, T) E^T[L(T - h, T) \times h]$$

$$= B(0, T) E^T \left[\frac{1}{B(T - h, T)} - \right]$$

The problem is the calculation of the expectation. Surprisingly, we already have enough information to calculate this expectation with construction of an explicit probability model. The one thing we know about this expectation is that under it all securities earn the same expected return over the period to T. So consider the strategy of buying a $T - h$-period zero and rolling over into the h-period zero. This strategy makes a solitary payment at T and its gross return is simply

$$\frac{1}{B(0, T - h)} \times \frac{1}{B(T - h, T)}$$

This gross return must have an expected value equal to that of the T-period zero. Thus

$$E^T \left[\frac{1}{B(0, T - h) \times B(T - h, T)} \right] = \frac{1}{B(0, T)}$$

Rearranging this formula gives

$$E^T \left[\frac{1}{B(T-h,T)} \right] = \frac{B(0,T-h)}{B(0,T)}$$

Replacing this expression in the valuation formula for the floating payment then gives

$$V_0 = B(0,T)E^T \left[\frac{1}{B(T-h,T)} - 1 \right]$$

$$= B(0,T) \left[\frac{B(0,T-h)}{B(0,T)} - 1 \right]$$

$$= B(0,T-h) - B(0,T)$$

This approach thus gives the same answer as from the replication analysis. Also note that the second line has the simple interpretation as the discounted value of the amount payable if the forward rate were to actually eventuate.

The result is that an alternative way of valuing perfect FRNs and by extension simple interest rate swaps is by valuing the floating payments as if they were fixed payments equal to h times the implied forward rate.

8.2.3   Valuing general FRNs

Consider a single floating payment in 2 years time that is equal to the prevailing annual spot rate on a 5 year zero. Labelling the spot rate in 2 years time on the 5 year zero by $R(2,7)$ we can write a valuation formula in terms of the T-measure probabilities where $T = 2$:

$$V_0 = B(0,2)E^T[R(2,7)]$$

The obvious problem is that we do not know the expectation of the 5 year spot rate. Now we know that the 5 year spot rate is a function of the 5 year zero price. In fact we know the exact formula

$$B(2,7) = \frac{1}{(1+R(2,7))^5}$$

$$R(2,7) = B(2,7)^{-1/5} - 1$$

and we label this function by

$$R(B_{2,7})$$

Now the key point is that although we do not know what the expected spot rate on the 5 year zero is, we do know what the expected price for the 5 year zero is. Consider buying a 7 year discount bond and then selling it after 2 years. The T-measure valuation formula tells us that

$$B(0,7) = \frac{E^T[B(2,7)]}{B(0,2)}$$

so the expected value that we label $\overline{B(2,7)}$ is given by

$$E^T[B(2,7)] = \frac{B(0,7)}{B(0,2)}$$

Now the relation between price and yield is convex, so that Jenson's inequality applies:

$$E^T[R(B_{2,7})] > R(E^T B(2,7))$$

We can now use a Taylor series expansion around this value (which is simply the forward price for a 5 year zero) within the valuation equation:

$$V_0 = B(0,2)E^T[R(\overline{B(2,7)}) + R'(\overline{B(2,7)})(B(2,7) - \overline{B(2,7)})]$$
$$+ B(0,2)E^T\left[\tfrac{1}{2}R''(\overline{B(2,7)})(B(2,7) - \overline{B(2,7)})^2\right]$$

Simplifying this gives

$$V_0 = B(0,2)R(\overline{B(2,7)}) + B(0,2)\tfrac{1}{2}R''(\overline{B(2,7)})E^T[(B(2,7) - \overline{B(2,7)})^2]$$

Now the first term is simply the discounted value of the expression $R(\overline{B(2,7)})$ and we can evaluate this expression using the formula for a spot rate and the expression for the forward price:

$$R(\overline{B(2,7)}) = \overline{B(2,7)}^{-1/5} - 1$$
$$= \left(\frac{B(0,7)}{B(0,2)}\right)^{-1/5} - 1$$

But this is simply the forward 5 year spot rate that we can call $F(0, R(2,7))$. Thus the first term values the floating payment simply as the discounted value of the payment equal to the implied forward rate — just the same as in the perfect FRN case. But now there is a second term. This second term is commonly referred to as the 'convexity' adjustment. We can calculate it in two ways. The first way is to directly evaluate the second derivative:

$$R(\overline{B(2,7)}) = (\overline{B(2,7)})^{-1/5} - 1$$

$$R'(\overline{B(2,7)}) = -\frac{1}{5}(\overline{B(2,7)})^{-6/5}$$

$$R''(\overline{B(2,7)}) = \frac{6}{25}(\overline{B(2,7)})^{-11/5}$$

$$= \frac{6}{25}(\overline{B(2,7)})^{-1/5}\frac{1}{(\overline{B(2,7)})^2}$$

Now we insert this back into the second term:

$$B(0,2)\frac{1}{2}R''(\overline{B(2,7)})E^T\left[(B(2,7) - \overline{B(2,7)})^2\right]$$

$$= B(0,2)\frac{3}{25}\overline{B(2,7)}^{-1/5}E^T\left[\left(\frac{B(2,7) - \overline{B(2,7)}}{\overline{B(2,7)}}\right)^2\right]$$

Now the expectation term is simply the proportional price variance (squared volatility) of the bond. Inserting some numbers into this expression will give some feel for the magnitude of the convexity adjustment. Assume the bond has annual proportional volatility of 10%. This gives a variance of 0.1^2 or 1%. Over two years the variance is doubled to 2%. I have ignored the pull-to-par phenomenon. Now let's assume a forward rate of 6%. This implies a forward price $\overline{B(2,7)}$ of $1.06^{-5} = 0.747$. The convexity adjustment is then given as

$$\frac{1}{2} \times \frac{6}{25} \times 0.747^{-1/5} \times 0.02 = 0.00254$$

This number is then added onto the discounted value of the forward rate to give the value of the coupon payment.

$$V_0 = P(0,2)(0.06 + 0.00254)$$

The result is that approximately 25 basis points needs to be added on to the forward rate to account for the convexity effect.

The tricky part in the above calculation was of the second derivative. This second derivative was of the yield–price function, rather than of the price–yield function, i.e. of

$$\frac{d^2r}{dP^2}$$

rather than the way we normally view things

$$\frac{d^2P}{dr^2}$$

The relation between the two derivatives is as follows:

$$\frac{d^2r}{dP^2} = \frac{d}{dP}\left(\frac{dP}{dr}\right)^{-1}$$

$$= -\left(\frac{dP}{dr}\right)^{-2}\frac{d}{dP}\left(\frac{dP}{dr}\right)$$

$$= -\left(\frac{dP}{dr}\right)^{-2}\frac{d^2P}{dr^2}\frac{dr}{dP}$$

$$= -\left(\frac{dP}{dr}\right)^{-3}\frac{d^2P}{dr^2}$$

We can express this as

$$P^2\frac{d^2r}{dP^2} = -\left(\frac{1}{P}\frac{dP}{dr}\right)^{-3}\left(\frac{1}{P}\frac{d^2P}{dr^2}\right)$$

$$= \frac{\text{Convexity}}{\text{Duration}^3}$$

And we can then use this in the convexity adjustment term:

$$\frac{1}{2}R''(\overline{B(2,7)})E^T[(B(2,7) - \overline{B(2,7)})^2]$$

$$= \frac{1}{2}\frac{\text{Convexity}}{\text{Duration}^3}E^T\left[\left(\frac{B(2,7) - \overline{B(2,7)}}{\overline{B(2,7)}}\right)^2\right]$$

Assuming convexity is 30 and duration is 5 the result is

$$\frac{1}{2}\frac{30}{125} \times 0.02 = 0.0024$$

That is the convexity adjustment results in the addition of 24 basis points onto the forward rate. The difference from the first analysis stems from the fact that we have not calculated duration and convexity on a modified basis, but this only makes a difference of around 1 basis point.

8.3   Further reading

Litterman, R., Scheinkman, J. and Weiss (1991) 'Volatility and the Yield Curve' *Journal of Fixed Income*.

8.4   Questions

1. A 20 year 8% annual coupon bond is selling at par. Calculate modified duration and convexity. The yield rises by 50 basis points. Calculate the new value by using (a) duration alone, (b) duration and convexity (c) full revaluation.

2. Value a payment to be received in 1 year's time equal to the prevailing yield on the US Treasury 30 year strip (notional principal $100 million). You estimate the 1 year forward 30 year rate to be 6%, and you estimate annual yield volatility of the 30 year discount bond to be 50 basis points.

Chapter 9

Callable and convertible bonds

Many corporate bonds, are subject to being *called*. The call feature gives the issuer of the bond the right to buy back the bond at a particular price. A schedule of prices and dates exist at which the bond can be called.

This right is an *option*, not an obligation so option valuation techniques need to be used in valuing callable bonds. Because the option cannot be separated from the corporate bond it is called an *embedded* option.

Since calling is a right of the issuer, the callable feature is a disadvantage to the investor and reduces the value of the bond. There are two related disadvantages for an investor. First, the issuer will call the bond if prevailing market yields are lower than the bond's coupon rate. The investor will then have to invest the proceeds at the prevailing lower market rates. The second disadvantage is the low potential for price appreciation in a falling rate environment. Since the bond can be called at a particular price, it cannot appreciate in price beyond this amount. Before we analyse the effect of callability in detail we first examine the common types of call provisions.

Of prime importance, is the amount of an issue that is callable. Sometimes the whole amount will be callable and other provisions allow for only a portion of the issue to be called. If the whole issue is not callable then the specific bonds which are called are selected either randomly or on a pro-rata basis. If the selection is random then the *Wall Street Journal* publishes the serial numbers of the certificates.

When callable bonds are issued there is often an interim period during which the bond is not callable. This feature is called *protection*, and it commonly takes two forms. *Refunding protection* is a form of call protection in which the issuer is not allowed to redeem the bonds by using lower cost debt financing. Note that the bonds can still be called, if the source of funds is not lower cost debt. For example, funds could be raised by asset sales, retained earnings, or seasoned equity offerings.

Call protection, is much stronger — it prevents the calling of the bonds, no matter what the source of refinancing.

The set of prices and dates at which a bond issue can be called is known as the *call schedule*. A typical call schedule, has higher prices (above par) at earlier dates, declining to par at dates further out.

Some corporate bonds have a *sinking fund provision*. A sinking fund provision *requires* the issuer to retire (pay back) a certain amount of debt each year. The debt that is to be retired is done so at face value. Note that this is not an option, so standard valuation techniques can be applied. Sometimes however, the issuer has the option to retire double the amount stipulated. This is called the *doubling option* and clearly requires option valuation techniques for valuation.

9.1   Valuing callable bonds

In order to value a callable bond we consider an identical non-callable bond. If the non-callable bond's price is above the call price, then the option to call is valuable. Issuer has a guaranteed buy low/sell high situation. But the callable bond will not increase in value to above the call price when rates fall because people know it will be called. The callable bond therefore has limited upside but normal downside. Accurate pricing of a callable bond is complicated by strategic issues of whether to call or not. Fortunately these issues are easily handled using a tree.

The essential pricing principle for callable bonds is the following

$$\text{Price(callable)} = \text{Price(non-callable)} - \text{Call value}$$

Thus a tree is built to value the non-callable bond. Then a tree is built for valuing the call option. Subtraction then gives the value of the callable bond.

9.1.1   Pricing the option to call

To value the option to call the backward induction approach must be used. Simply using state prices (multiply and add) does not work as it ignores the strategic issues of whether to call or not. The problem is a reasonably sophisticated problem, in that we need to model the behaviour of the issuer in deciding whether or not to call the bond. The starting assumption is that the issuer is *rational* and maximizes the value of his call option by pursuing an optimal call policy. Our problem is model this optimal call policy. In any period (if the bond has not already been called) the issuer has to decide whether or not to call the bond. Obviously if the non-callable bond is selling for less than the call price, the bond should not be called. It is when the non-callable bond is selling for more than the call price that the decision is difficult. In this situation the option is *in-the-money* and calling may seem optimal. This is not necessarily the case, since by holding on a period, the option may end up further in the money, with a greater value when exercised later. The tricky part of valuation is to model this strategic decision-making.

Somewhat surprisingly, this type of problem is handled easily using a tree and the principle of backward induction. In reality we are going to use a simple form of dynamic programming. Dynamic programming works by breaking complex multi-period problems up into a number of simple one-period problems. The one-period problem we face here is a simple binary decision — whether to exercise the option (call the bond) or whether to hold.

Recall that backward induction starts at the final date — the bond's maturity date. At maturity the option to call is worth zero. At the previous period, the issuer may either exercise the option or he may simply hold the option. The value from holding is found from backward induction. The value from exercising is the difference between the non-callable price and the call price.

The general formula is

$$V(t,j) = \max(V_h, V_e)$$

where

$$V_h = \frac{0.5V(t+1, j+1) + 0.5V(t+1, j-1)}{1 + r_{t,j}\Delta}$$

$$V_e = \text{Price(non-callable)} - \text{Call price}$$

The above formula, though very simple and easy to implement via a binomial tree, is actually quite sophisticated as it captures and prices the optimal calling strategy of the issuer. By working backwards through the tree applying this formula at all points, a call option value will be reached that reflects the pursuance of an optimal exercise strategy.

This formula is applied recursively back through the tree to give a current value of the option to call. Subtracting this value from the price of the non-callable bond then gives the value of the callable bond.

As a very simple example we consider a 2 year zero-coupon corporate bond that is callable in 1 year's time at 90. We construct a 1 year rate tree that prices correctly the otherwise identical non-callable.

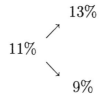

Year 0   Year 1

This implies the following tree for the price of the otherwise identical non-callable:

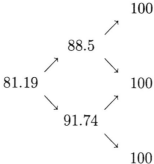

Year 0   Year 1   Year 2

We now value the option to call the bond, by using the backward valuation formula:

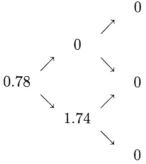

Year 0   Year 1   Year 2

The value of the option to call the bond is $0.78 so we can price the callable bond as $80.41 = 81.19 − 0.78.

9.1.2 Price behaviour of a callable bond

Several key features of the price behaviour of a callable bond can be illustrated through the following stylized example. Consider an 8% coupon 30 year bond that is callable at par in 3 years time. We are interested in how the price of this bond will respond to changes in current spot rates. We make the simplifying assumption that the spot rate is flat and shifts in a parallel fashion.

The starting point for analysis is to plot the price–yield relationships for a non-callable 30 year 8% coupon bond, and for a non-callable 3 year 8% coupon bond. This is shown in the following figure.

Price is shown on the vertical axis and yield on the horizontal axis. The steeper line is the price of the 30 year non-callable coupon bond, and the flatter line is the price of the 3 year non-callable coupon bond. Since there is only one exercise date — in 3 years — the call decision is very simple. The issuer will call if the price of the non-callable is greater than par — the call price. If we knew the bond was going to be called then we know it would be, in effect only a 3 year bond. If we knew that it was not going to be called then the bond would be in effect a 30 year non-callable bond.

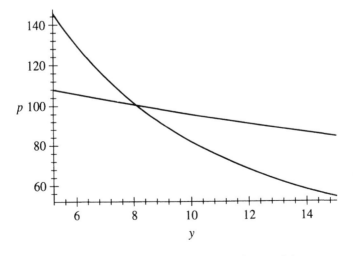

Figure 9.1 30 year and 3 year bonds: price–yield relationships

This means that the callable bond's price must be below the price of both the 3 year and the 30 year non-callable bonds. Why? Imagine, if the issuer had to state now whether or not it would be called. In effect this amount to choosing whether the bond will be a 3 year or a 30 year bond. The issuer will choose the cheaper of the two and this would result in the price being given by the lower of the 3 year and 30 year prices. As the issuer can in reality decide not now but in 3 years (i.e. he has more flexibility) this can only add to the value of the call feature, and thus reduce the value of the callable bond.

This implies that as rates decrease the price of the bond will approach that of a 3 year bond. As rates rise the price of the callable will approach the price of the 30 year non-callable bond.

An interesting point to note is that the callable bond can have a region of negative convexity. That is as rates rise, the bond value becomes increasingly sensitive to yield changes as it behaves more like a 30 year bond than a 3 year bond.

9.2   Convertible bonds

The conversion feature of a convertible bond allows the holder of a convertible bond to convert the bonds into a predetermined number of shares of common stock of the issuer. Since convertibility is an option not an obligation, option techniques are required for valuing convertibles. Before analysing valuation, we look briefly at the common features of convertible bonds.

The number of shares of common stock that will be received per bond on conversion is called the *conversion ratio*. It need not be constant over time. The *Par conversion price* is simply

$$\frac{\text{Par value of convertible}}{\text{Conversion ratio}}$$

and this is the 'price' at which stock can effectively be bought for, assuming that the bond trades at par at conversion.

The *Conversion value* of a convertible bond is the value of the bond if converted into stock and is given by

$$\text{Price of stock} \times \text{Conversion ratio}$$

This ignores *dilution effects* which we examine later. The *straight value* of a convertible, is the value of the otherwise identical non-convertible bond.

You should convince yourself that a convertible should never sell for less than the greater of the straight value and the convertible value.

The *Market conversion price* is the price effectively paid for common stock if convertibles are bought and immediately converted. The formula is

$$\text{Market conversion price} = \frac{\text{Price of convertible}}{\text{Conversion ratio}}$$

Since the market conversion price must be at least as high as the market share price, we can define the market conversion premium as

$$\text{Market conversion premium} = \text{Market conversion price} - \text{Share price}$$

This premium reflects the option value of the convertibility feature, and is sometimes expressed as a ratio:

$$\text{Market conversion premium ratio} = \frac{\text{Market conversion premium}}{\text{Share price}}$$

9.2.1   Dilution

In the above we have ignored possible effects resulting from *dilution* of the company's worth following conversion. We can define a *dilution factor a* as

$$\text{Dilution factor } (a)$$
$$= \frac{\# \text{ Convertibles} \times \text{Conversion ratio}}{\# \text{ Existing shares} + (\# \text{ Convertibles} \times \text{Conversion ratio})}$$

The top line gives the number of new shares that come into existence as a result of conversion, and the bottom line gives the total number of shares after conversion.

9.2.2   Value at maturity

Let V_T be the value of the firm after the last coupon has been paid. If bond holders convert they forgo their principal payment with a total aggregate value say of F, and in return they receive a fraction of the value of the firm given as

$$\text{Dilution factor} \times V_T$$

Thus they will not convert unless

$$\text{Dilution factor} \times V_T > F$$

In fact, we can calculate the aggregate value C_T of convertibles at maturity in terms of three scenarios:

$$C_T = \begin{cases} V_T & \text{if } V_T < F \\ F & \text{if } F < V_T > F/a \\ aV_T & \text{if } V_T > F/a \end{cases}$$

In the first scenario, the value of the firm is so low that the firm defaults and the convertible bond holders are not even fully paid their principal. In the second scenario, no conversion takes place, the firm does not default, and the convertible bond holders get their principal payment. In the third scenario, the firm has done well, and conversion takes place. The convertible holders get a fraction (the dilution factor) of the value of the firm.

9.2.3   General valuation

The structure of the payoffs of the convertible at maturity can be easily seen in Figure 9.2. This diagram also provides the key to valuing simple convertibles. The key is to note that a convertible security can be thought of as the sum of two parts — a straight corporate bond, and a call (actually a warrant) with strike price F/a. The actual formula for the aggregate value of convertibles is

$$\text{Value of straight bond} + \text{value of warrant}$$

$$= \text{Value of bond} + aC(V_0, F/a, T, \sigma)$$

where $C(V_0, F/a, T, \sigma)$ is the Black–Scholes option price for a call option with strike F/a, maturity T, and volatility of firm value given by σ. Note that the current price V_0 is the current value of the firm and this equals the value of equity plus the value of convertibles. The formula is not circular however since we can solve the formula for a unique value of convertibles.

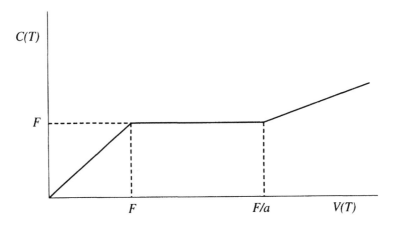

Figure 9.2 Stucture of the payoffs at maturity

9.3   Further reading

1. Nyborg, K. (1996) 'The Use and Pricing of Convertible Bonds,' *Applied Mathematical Finance*, 1996.

9.4   Questions

1. 'Comparing a callable bond to the otherwise identical non-callable bond, the callable bond is riskier since it has the added risk of being called.' Agree, disagree, why?

Chapter 10

Credit risk

So far all analysis has presumed an effective enforcement mechanism for the payment of promised cash flows. In the real world the promise of a payment and actual payment are two different things. In the real world firms can default on their obligations. How can we value securities which may default?

Default has two forms. First the traded securities may be the bonds for example of a firm which may default. The price of the bonds must then incorporate an assessment of the likelihood of default. The other situation arises even when the underlying security is default free. For example if an option on a Treasury bond is an OTC (over-the-counter) option then we may be exposed to the default of our counterparty. This is called counterparty risk.

In the following we first discuss the role of credit analysis and the credit rating agencies. We then describe the two approaches that have been taken to the formal modelling of credit risk — the *firm value* approach; and the default probability approach. We then look at a simple example of the latter approach.

10.1 Credit ratings

Most large investment banks and some institutional investors have their own credit analysis departments, whose role is to assess the creditworthiness of companies. Most investors however, rely on the ratings supplied by commercial rating companies. The two largest such companies are Moody's Investor Services, and Standard & Poor's Corporation. Both companies employ a system of bond ratings, where *highest grade* refers to those companies whose bonds are the least likely to default.

Moody's assigns the highest grade bonds a rating of Aaa, and Standard and Poor's use the letters AAA (both are referred to as triple A). The next grade is Aa or AA (double A), and the third grade is assigned A by both agencies. The next three grades are Baa or BBB; Ba or BB, and B (used by both agencies). Standard and Poor's use a + or − sign to provide a more accurate breakdown within classes, and Moody's use the numbers 1, 2, and 3 for the same purposes.

One approach to modelling credit risk is to construct models in which firms have probabilities of switching between various rating levels. These probabilities can be inferred from historical data on rating upgrades and downgrades.

10.2   A model of credit risk

We now outline a relatively simple model of credit risk based on the paper by Jarrow, Lando, and Turnbull (1997) which has the following features:

1. Debt of different seniorities from the one firm can be incorporated via different recovery rates.

2. The model can be built upon any term-structure model, such as Ho–Lee, Black–Derman–Toy, etc.

3. It incorporates historical data on downgrades and upgrades to determine the risk-neutral probabilities of default.

4. It can be used to price and hedge options on risky debt or credit derivatives.

10.2.1   The basic setup

We start by assuming that we have a complete set of default-free discount bonds with prices denoted $B(0, t)$. We also have a default-free money-market account that accumulates at the one-period (cc) rate:

$$\mathcal{M}_t = \exp\left(\sum_{i=1}^{t-1} r_i\right)$$

We denote by $v(t, T)$ the time t price of a risky discount bond promising to pay one dollar at time T. If the firm that has issued this bond is bankrupt at time T then full payment will not be made; instead partial payment of δ the default recovery rate, is paid per dollar promised. Recall that the price of a default-free discount bond is given by the backward valuation formula, under the risk-neutral probabilities as

$$B(0, T) = E[\mathcal{M}_t^{-1}]$$

The price of a risky bond can be expressed as

$$v(0, T) = E[\mathcal{M}_t^{-1}(\delta 1(\text{bankruptcy}) + 1(\text{no bankruptcy}))]$$

where $1(.)$ is a random variable called an indicator function that takes the value 1 if the event is true and 0 otherwise.

We now assume that the process for interest rates (and hence for the money-market account) is independent of the bankruptcy process. We can thus separate the valuation formula as

$$v(0, T) = E[\mathcal{M}_t^{-1}]E(\delta 1(\text{bankruptcy}) + 1(\text{no bankruptcy}))$$
$$= B(0, T)(\delta \Pr(\text{bankruptcy}) + 1(1 - \Pr(\text{bankruptcy})))$$

The term structure of credit-risky debt is thus determined by the default-free term structure and the probability of bankruptcy occurring before specified dates. We now examine how we can model these probabilities of bankruptcy.

10.2.2   Credit ratings and default probabilities

The bankruptcy process is modelled by a *Markov* chain, in which a firm switches between various rating levels (the worst of which is bankruptcy) with various transition probabilities. Formally we have k *states*, one corresponding to each rating level, and a final kth state corresponding to bankruptcy. The transition probabilities are laid out in a $k \times k$ transition matrix Q.

$$Q = \begin{bmatrix} q_{11} & q_{12} & & q_{1k} \\ q_{21} & q_{22} & & q_{2k} \\ & & & \\ 0 & 0 & 0 & 1 \end{bmatrix}$$

The matrix is read as follows, the ijth element (in row i column j) gives the probability of a firm going from state i to state j over one period. The final row consisting of zeros and a one, states that if a firm is in bankruptcy it will stay that way for certain. The last column shows the probabilities of firms in each class becoming bankrupt over the next period. Estimates of this matrix for a time period of 1 year can be obtained from Standard and Poor's and Moody's.

The beauty of the Markov approach is that transition probabilities for n periods are easily obtained. The transition matrix for n periods is simply

$$Q_{0,n} = Q^n$$

$$= \overbrace{Q \times Q \times \cdots \times Q}^{n}$$

10.2.3 Risk-neutral default probabilities

The above transition probabilities are historical ('actual' probabilities) not risk-neutral probabilities. We transform these probabilities to risk-neutral probabilities $\widetilde{Q}_{t,t+1}$ in the following way.

$$\widetilde{Q}_{t,t+1} = \mathbf{I} + \Pi(t)(Q - \mathbf{I})$$

where $\mathbf{I}$ is the identity matrix:

$$\mathbf{I} = \begin{bmatrix} 1 & 0 & 0 & 0 \\ 0 & 1 & 0 & 0 \\ 0 & 0 & \ddots & 0 \\ 0 & 0 & 0 & 1 \end{bmatrix}$$

and

$$\Pi(t) = \begin{bmatrix} \Pi_1(t) & 0 & 0 & 0 & 0 \\ 0 & \Pi_2(t) & 0 & 0 & 0 \\ 0 & 0 & \ddots & 0 & 0 \\ 0 & 0 & 0 & \Pi_{k-1}(t) & 0 \\ 0 & 0 & 0 & 0 & 1 \end{bmatrix}$$

a diagonal matrix with diagonal elements that can be time-dependent. The diagonal elements $\Pi_i(t)$ have the interpretation of being risk premiums that adjust actual probabilities to risk-neutral probabilities.

10.2.4   The probability of default

We can now calculate the probability of default. We first calculate the n-period risk-neutral transition matrix as

$$\widetilde{Q}_{0,n} = \widetilde{Q}_{0,1} \times \widetilde{Q}_{1,2} \times \cdots \times \widetilde{Q}_{n-1,n}$$

Starting from a particular rating, the risk-neutral probability of default happening by the nth period is given by the final element in the ith row of the matrix $\widetilde{Q}_{0,n}$. We are thus able to compute the probability of default over any time horizon starting from any particular rating level.

We can then write the risky bond pricing formula as

$$v(0,T) = B(0,T)(\delta \widetilde{q}_{i,k}(0,T) + 1(1 - \widetilde{q}_{i,k}(0,T)))$$

where $\widetilde{q}_{i,k}(0,T)$ is the element in row i, column k of the T-period risk-neutral probability matrix

$$\widetilde{Q}_{0,T}$$

The above formula can be used to derive explicit expressions for forward rates on risky debt, and for the spread between forwards on risky and default-free debt.

10.2.5   Fitting risky zero-coupon bonds

Given historical data on credit class transitions, the only additional information the above approach requires is the risk premia $\Pi(t)$. These can be inferred from the prices of corporate bonds. The key relation we need can be derived from the following equation:

$$\Pr(\text{bankruptcy}) = \frac{B(0,T) - v(0,T)}{B(0,T)} \times \frac{1}{1 - \delta}$$

where bankruptcy refers to bankruptcy during any period in $(0, T)$. We build up our estimates in a recursive manner, similar to bootstrapping zero-coupon rates. We have that $\Pr(\text{bankruptcy})$ in the first period for a bond of rating level i is given by the final element in the ith row of the matrix:

$$\widetilde{Q}_{0,1} = I + \Pi(0)(Q - I)$$

so the diagonal elements of $\Pi(0)$ can be chosen so as to match the 1 year yields of bonds in each credit class. One then proceeds along the yield curve choosing the elements of Π so as to match corporate bond yields.

10.2.6   Options and credit derivatives

The paper by Jarrow, Lando, and Turnbull shows how this model can be combined with a term-structure model of default-free rates to generate a relatively simple way of pricing and hedging options on credit-risky bonds and credit derivatives.

10.3   Further reading

Jarrow, Lando, and Turnbull (1997) 'A Markov Model for the Term Structure of Credit Risk Spreads' *Review of Financial Studies* 10(2).

Chapter 11

Continuous-time finance

In this section we introduce the basic techniques and concepts of stochastic calculus as used in finance. Many papers in the non-academic investment literature (such as *Financial Analysts' Journal, Journal of Derivatives, Journal of Fixed Income*, and *Risk*) use the techniques of stochastic calculus. Thus the ability to work with, or at least understand stochastic calculus, is essential if one is to keep abreast of new developments. This paper introduces some of the basic analytical methods commonly used to specify interest rate and term structure processes. It is only an introduction designed as a starting point for people who wish to understand this area. A list of references for further study is provided at the end of the chapter.

11.1 The basics

11.1.1 Standard Wiener processes

Consider a random walk in discrete time:

$$W(t+1) = W(t) + e(t+1)$$

$$W(0) = W_0$$

$$e \sim i.i.d. \quad N(0,1)$$

In words this means that the value of W changes randomly through time. It starts at some fixed value W_0 and takes on new values at the integers $1, 2, \ldots$. The rule for evolution is simple. The new value simply equals the old value plus a disturbance e that is random (or *stochastic*). This random term

143

is a normally distributed random variable with mean of zero and variance of one. Each disturbance is independent of all other disturbances at other times (iid means independently and identically distributed as). The fact that the process is discrete means that W is undefined between integer values of time — it is only defined at the integer values.

W_t is called a random walk because it appears that W wanders aimlessly taking random steps up and down. Now we are interested in what happens between the integer values, but we still wish to preserve the random nature of the process. Consider the following process:

$$W(t + \Delta) = W(t) + e(t + \Delta)$$

$$W(0) = W_0$$

$$e \sim i.i.d. \quad N(0, \Delta)$$

This process differs from the first, in that where a 1 appeared in the first process, a Δ appears now. Thus the time increment is not one but Δ. The key point is that the variance of the disturbance is not 1 but is Δ. Think of a single time period of unit length now being split up into n sub-periods. If we define $\Delta = 1/n$, then some algebra shows that the new process has the same variance over n periods (i.e. variance of 1) as the first process did over one period.

$$\text{Var} \ (W(t + 1) - W(t)) = \text{Var} \ [e(t + \Delta) + e(t + 2\Delta) + \cdots + e(t + n\Delta)]$$

$$= \text{Var} \ [e(t + \Delta)] + \cdots + \text{Var} \ [e(t + n\Delta)]$$

$$= n \times \Delta = n \times \frac{1}{n} = 1$$

Now consider the process as Δ becomes very small $\Delta \to dt$:

$$W(t + dt) = W(t) + e(t + dt)$$

$$e \sim i.i.d. \quad N(0, dt)$$

and define

$$dW(t) = W(t + dt) - W(t)$$

$$dW \sim iid \quad N(0, dt)$$

It will be extremely helpful to think of dt as a very small number so that $dt^a = 0$, whenever $a > 1$. We can think of dW as a normally distributed random variable with mean of zero and variance dt. The process $W(t)$ is called a standard Weiner process, and is characterized by the following three properties:

1. W_t is almost surely continuous, with $W_0 = 0$.
2. W_t has independent increments, so that for successive times p, q, r, s we have that $(W_q - W_p)$ is independent of $(W_s - W_r)$.
3. $W_t - W_s$ is normally distributed with mean zero and variance $t - s$.

11.1.2   Ito multiplication

The following three properties of standard Weiner processes are vital:

1. $dt^2 = 0$
2. $dW(t)dt = 0$
3. $dW(t)^2 = dt$

Table 11.1 shows these results in multiplication table format.

Since these properties are so important, and to aid in understanding and memorizing these laws, we provide simple heuristic 'proofs'. The proofs rely mainly on the probability law:

$$\text{Var } (x) = E[x^2] - (E[x])^2$$

The first property follows directly from the definition of dt as a very small number so that $dt^a = 0$, whenever $a > 1$. The next two are proved in the same way. We first show that the expected value of the LHS of the equation equals the RHS. We then show that the variance of the LHS term is zero so that the equality must hold without the expectation, as the LHS is non-random. For **2** we have that $E[dW(t)dt] = E[dW(t)]\, dt = 0 \cdot dt = 0$. Now the

Table 11.1 Ito multiplication table

×	dW	dt
dW	dt	0
dt	0	0

variance of $dW(t)dt$ is given by

$$\text{Var}\,(dW(t)dt) = E[dW(t)^2 dt^2] - (E[dW(t)dt])^2$$
$$= E[dW(t)^2 \cdot 0] - 0^2$$
$$= 0$$

For number **3** we have that the expectation of $dW(t)^2$ is dt since this expectation is the variance of $dW(t)$, which is defined as dt. The variance is given by

$$\text{Var}\,(dW(t)^2) = E[dW(t)^4] - (E[dW(t)^2])^2$$
$$= 3dt^2 - dt^2 = 0$$

where the first term in the second line comes from the fact that for a normal random variable $z \sim N(0, \sigma^2)$ the expectation of z^4 is three times the variance:

$$E[z^4] = 3\sigma^2$$

11.1.3   Generalized Weiner processes

We now consider the *generalized Weiner process*:

$$dX = a(.)dt + b(.)dW$$

Note first that we have dropped the subscript t, as time dependence is assumed to be understood. Starting from the end we know that dW is a normally distributed random variable with mean zero and variance dt. dX is also a random variable, being a linear combination of a random variable and a constant. The random variable dX has mean $a(.)dt$ and variance $b(.)^2 dt$. Thus by varying a and b we can vary the mean and variance of dX. More accurately we call a the 'drift' of the process and b the (instantaneous) volatility. Note that variance is the square of volatility.

Example — Arithmetic Brownian motion

$$dX = \alpha\,dt + \sigma\,dW$$

This process is called arithmetic Brownian motion with drift α and volatility σ. X has the following properties:

1. X may be positive or negative.

2. The distribution of future values of X at date $u > t$, conditional upon X_t is normal with mean $X_t + \alpha(u - t)$ and standard deviation $\sigma\sqrt{u - t}$.

Example — Geometric Brownian motion

$$dX = \alpha X \, dt + \sigma X \, dW$$

Note that geometric Brownian motion has drift and volatility proportional to the current value of the process X. Nonetheless with this process we still say the drift is α and the volatility is σ. Geometric Brownian motion has the following properties:

1. If X starts at a positive value it will remain positive.

2. X has an *absorbing barrier* at zero, so that if the process should hit zero it will remain there.

3. The conditional distribution of X_u given X_t is lognormal. Thus $\ln X_u$ is distributed normally with conditional mean $\ln X_t + \alpha(u - t) - \frac{1}{2}\sigma^2(u - t)$ and conditional standard deviation $\sigma\sqrt{u - t}$.

Stock prices

The standard model for a stock price process, is that the price S_t follows a Weiner process. A useful way of expressing this is to say that S_t is a solution to the following stochastic differential equation:

$$\frac{dS_t}{S_t} = \mu_t \, dt + \sigma_t \, dW_t$$

The drift term μ_t is now called the *instantaneous expected return* and the volatility term σ_t is called the *instantaneous volatility*. If the drift and volatility terms are constant or are specified exogenously (i.e. non-random) then the solution to the above process can be represented as

$$S_t = S_0 \exp\left[\int_{s=0}^{t} \mu_s \, ds\right] \exp\left[\int_{s=0}^{t} \sigma_s \, dW_s - \frac{1}{2}\int_{s=0}^{t} \sigma_s^2 \, ds\right]$$

This expression results from Ito's lemma, which is the most important result in this area.

11.2   Ito's lemma

Ito's lemma provides us with a description of the process followed by a *function* of a Weiner process. If f is a function of one variable with continuous first and second derivatives f' and f'' and X_t is a generalized Weiner process

$$dX = a_t\, dt + b_t\, dW$$

then Ito's lemma states that the process f_t defined by the value of the function at X_t denoted $f(X_t)$ follows the following stochastic differential equation (sde):

$$df_t = \left(f'_t a_t + \tfrac{1}{2} f''_t b_t^2 \right) dt + f'_t b_t\, dW_t$$

This result is extremely useful as it provides a formula for the function of any Ito process. We can better understand this formula if we 'derive' it as a Taylor series expansion

$$f(X + dX) = f(X) + \frac{\partial f}{\partial X}\, dX + \frac{1}{2} \frac{\partial^2 f}{\partial X^2}(dX)^2 \quad \text{or}$$

$$df(X) = \frac{\partial f}{\partial X}\, dX + \frac{1}{2} \frac{\partial^2 f}{\partial X^2}(dX)^2$$

and then use the three rules of Ito multiplication:

$$(dX)^2 = (a_t\, dt + b_t\, dW)^2$$

$$= a_t^2\, dt^2 + b_t^2\, dW^2 + 2a_t\, dt \cdot b_t\, dW$$

$$= b_t^2 \cdot dt$$

This then gives

$$df(X) = \frac{\partial f}{\partial X}\, dX + \frac{1}{2} \frac{\partial^2 f}{\partial X^2} b_t^2 \cdot dt$$

$$= \frac{\partial f}{\partial X}(a_t\, dt + b_t\, dW) + \frac{1}{2} \frac{\partial^2 f}{\partial X^2} b_t^2 \cdot dt$$

Now collect terms with dt and terms with dW:

$$df(X) = \left(\frac{\partial f}{\partial X} a_t + \frac{1}{2} \frac{\partial^2 f}{\partial X^2} b_t^2 \right) dt + \frac{\partial f}{\partial X} b_t\, dW$$

If the function also depends on time t, then we write Ito's lemma as:

$$df(X,t) = \frac{\partial f}{\partial t} dt + \frac{\partial f}{\partial X} dX + \frac{1}{2} \frac{\partial^2 f}{\partial X^2} (dX)^2$$

The derivatives $\frac{\partial f}{\partial X}$, $\frac{\partial f}{\partial t}$, $\frac{\partial^2 f}{\partial X^2}$, are calculated in the normal way, as first and second derivatives. The terms dX and $(dX)^2$ are calculated again using the three rules of multiplication.

$$df(X,t) = \left[\frac{\partial f}{\partial t} + \frac{\partial f}{\partial X} a(.) + \frac{1}{2} \frac{\partial^2 f}{\partial X^2} b^2(.) \right] dt + \frac{\partial f}{\partial X} b(.) dW$$

Note that the basic form is the same. We have a drift term (in square brackets) and we have a random term ending in dW.

With two Wiener processes:

$$dX = \mu_x \, dt + \sigma_x \, dW^x$$

$$dY = \mu_y \, dt + \sigma_y \, dW^y$$

where dW^x and dW^y have correlation ρ_{xy} defined by

$$dW^x \cdot dW^y = \rho_{xy} \, dt$$

we have that a function defined on these two processes $f(X,Y)$ follows the process

$$df = f_x \, dX + f_y \, dY + \tfrac{1}{2} f_{xx} (dX)^2 + \tfrac{1}{2} f_{yy} (dY)^2 + f_{xy} \, dX \, dY$$

where subscripts represent derivatives, e.g. $f_{xx} = \frac{\partial^2 f}{dX^2}$. Two particularly useful instances of this law are the **product law**

$$\frac{d(XY)}{XY} = \left(\frac{dX}{X} \right) + \left(\frac{dY}{Y} \right) + \left(\frac{dX}{X} \cdot \frac{dY}{Y} \right)$$

and the **ratio law**

$$\frac{d(X/Y)}{X/Y} = \left(\frac{dX}{X} \right) - \left(\frac{dY}{Y} \right) + \left(\frac{dY}{Y} \right)^2 - \left(\frac{dX}{X} \right) \left(\frac{dY}{Y} \right)$$

11.3   Martingales

A martingale is a process which provides a mathematical characterization of a 'fair' game. It is a process for which the expected future value is simply the current value. That is a process M_t such that

$$E_t[M_t] = m_t, \qquad T > t$$

A process is *adapted* to the filtration generated by a Wiener process if its random value at time t can be determined from the history of the Weiner process up to that time. If B_t is an adapted process for t in $(0, T)$, then the process

$$dM_t = B_t \, dW_t$$

is a martingale (leaving aside questions of existence). At $t = 0$, $M_0 = 0$, we have that $E_0[M_t] = 0$.

A useful characterization of a martingale is as a process with a zero drift term. Some examples of continuous martingales based on Wiener processes are:

1. W_t itself;

2. $W_t^2 - t$; and

3. $W_t^3 - 3tW_t$.

The results can be illustrated using Ito's lemma and the zero drift condition for martingales. Let

$$Y_t = W_t^2 - t$$

then

$$dY_t = \frac{dY}{dt} dt + \frac{dY}{dW} \cdot dW + \frac{1}{2} \frac{d^2Y}{dW^2} dt$$

$$= -1dt + \frac{1}{2} \cdot 2dt + 2W_t \, dW_t$$

$$= 0 \cdot dt + 2W_t \, dW_t$$

thus satisfying the zero drift condition. For **3** let

$$Z_t = W_t^3 - 3tW_t$$

then

$$dZ_t = \frac{dZ}{dt}\,dt + \frac{dZ}{dW}\,dW + \frac{1}{2}\frac{d^2Z}{dW^2}\,dW^2$$

$$= -3W_t\,dt + 3W_t^2\,dW + \frac{1}{2}6W_t\,dt$$

$$= 0\cdot dt + 3W_t^2\,dW$$

A very general result is that for any constant c the process $X_t = \exp\left[cW_t - \frac{1}{2}c^2t\right]$ is a martingale:

$$dX_t = \frac{dW}{dt}dt + \frac{dX}{dW}\,dW + \frac{1}{2}\frac{d^2X}{dW^2}\,dt$$

$$= -\frac{1}{2}c^2\exp\left[cW_t - \frac{1}{2}c^2t\right]dt + c\exp\left[cW_t - \frac{1}{2}c^2t\right]dW$$

$$+ \frac{1}{2}c^2\exp\left[cW_t - \frac{1}{2}c^2t\right]dt$$

$$= -\frac{1}{2}c^2X_t\,dt + \frac{1}{2}c^2X_t\,dt + cX_t\,dW$$

$$= 0\cdot dt + cX_t\,dW$$

Another way of generating martingales is via defining a variable in terms of an expectation. For example consider a process Z_t. Now define the process $M_t = E_t[Z_T]$. This satisfies the martingale property since for u in (t, T).

$$E_t[M_u] = E_t[E_u[Z_T]] = E_t[Z_T] = M_t$$

This follows from the law of iterated expectations, which says that you can't expect to change your expectation!

11.4   The market risk premium or the continuous-time APT

Assume we have N assets whose prices are adapted to a set of N independent Wiener processes $W_t = (W_t^1, W_t^2, \ldots, W_t^N)$. A typical asset will have price process

$$\frac{dS_t^j}{S_t^j} = \mu_t^j\,dt + \sum_{i=1}^{N}\sigma_t^{ji}\,dW_t^i$$

$$= \mu_t^j\,dt + \sigma_t^j\,dW_t$$

where $\sigma_t^j \, dW_t$ represents the summation across the Wiener processes and σ_t^j is therefore an N-vector. Now to prevent arbitrage the expected return of an asset must be linearly related to the risks that the asset is subject to. But all risk sensitivities are summarized by the vector σ_t^j. Thus the expected return must have the APT form:

$$\mu_t^j = r_t + \sum_{i=1}^{N} \lambda_t^i \sigma_t^{ji}$$

$$= r_t + \lambda_t \sigma_t^j$$

for all assets j. The vector λ_t is called the market price of risk vector and is, of course the same for all assets. r_t is the definite rate of return available from a risk-free investment over a very short period. The return is adapted to the set of Wiener processes.

11.5   The risk-neutral measure

We define a *money-market process* B_t which represents the value at time t of a savings account which earns interest at the short rate r_t and from which no withdrawals or deposits are made. Thus

$$B_t = \exp \int_0^t r_s \, ds$$

and

$$\frac{dB_t}{B_t} = r_t \, dt$$

The key idea which we wish to show is that by a suitable change of probability measure the ratio S_t/B_t will be a martingale. We first use the ratio rule to calculate the process followed by the ratio:

$$\frac{d(S_t/B_t)}{S_t/B_t} = \left(\frac{dS}{S} \right) - \left(\frac{dB}{B} \right) + \left(\frac{dB}{B} \right)^2 - \left(\frac{dS}{S} \right) \left(\frac{dB}{B} \right)$$

$$= \left(r_t + \sum_{i=1}^{N} \lambda_t^i \sigma_t^{ji} \right) dt + \sum_{i=1}^{N} \sigma_t^{ji} \, dW_t^i - r_t \, dt$$

$$= \sum_{i=1}^{N} \sigma_t^{ji} (dW_t^i + \lambda_t^i \, dt)$$

Now construct a martingale based on the market risk premium:

$$m_t = \exp\left[-\int_{s=0}^{t} \lambda_s \, dW_s - \frac{1}{2} \int_{s=0}^{t} \lambda_s^2 \, ds\right]$$

Applying Ito's lemma we get

$$dm_t = \frac{dm_t}{dt} \, dt + \frac{dm_t}{dW} \, dW_t + \frac{1}{2} \frac{d^2 m}{dW^2} \, dt$$

$$= -\frac{1}{2} \lambda_t^2 m_t \, dt - m_t \lambda_t \, dW_t + \frac{1}{2} \lambda_t^2 m_t \, dt$$

$$= -m_t \lambda_t \, dW_t$$

thus showing the driftless condition of a martingale.

Now if we use the product rule we can show that $m_t(S_t/B_t)$ is a martingale:

$$\frac{d(m_t(S_t/B_t))}{m_t(S_t/B_t)} = \left(\frac{dm}{m}\right) + \left(\frac{d(S_t/B_t)}{S_t/B_t}\right) + \left(\frac{dm}{m}\right)\left(\frac{d(S_t/B_t)}{S_t/B_t}\right)$$

$$= \lambda_t \, dW_t + \sum_{i=1}^{N} \sigma_t^{ji} \left(dW_t^i + \lambda_t^i \, dt\right) + \lambda_t \, dW_t \sum_{i=1}^{N} \sigma_t^{ji}(dW_t^i + \lambda_t^i \, dt)$$

$$= 0 \cdot dt + \sum_{i=1}^{N} (\sigma_t^{ji} - \lambda_t^i) \, dW_t^i$$

Thus we have that $m_t(S_t/B_t)$ is a martingale so that

$$\frac{m_t S_t}{B_t} = E_t\left[\frac{m_T S_T}{B_T}\right]$$

Since m_t is also a martingale we can write this as

$$\frac{S_t}{B_t} = \frac{E_t\left[\dfrac{m_T S_T}{B_T}\right]}{E_t[m_T]}$$

$$= E_t\left[\frac{m_T}{E_t[m_T]}\left(\frac{S_T}{B_T}\right)\right]$$

Now multiplication by the term $\frac{m_T}{E_t[m_T]}$, when m_t is a non-negative martingale amounts to a *change of measure*. We write expectations under the new *risk-neutral* measure as E^B and define the change by

$$E_t^B[X_T] = E_t \left[\frac{m_T}{E_t[m_T]} X_T \right]$$

The superscript B reminds us that all assets expressed as ratios over the money-market account are martingales under this measure. We thus have that

$$\frac{S_t}{B_t} = E_t^B \left(\frac{S_T}{B_T} \right)$$

so that the ratio S_t/B_t is a martingale in the risk-neutral measure.

11.6   Change of probability measure

We mentioned previously the T-measure. How do we derive this measure from the risk-neutral measure? The answer to this question and ones like it is given from the following change of measure formula. We define a new measure with reference to an asset Z by

$$E_t^Z[X_T] = E_t^B \left[\left(\frac{Z_T/B_T}{E_t^B[Z_T/B_T]} \right) X_T \right]$$

which, since $E_t^B[Z_T/B_T] = Z_t/B_t$, can be written as

$$Z_t E_t^Z[X_T] = B_t E_t^B \left[(Z_T/B_T) X_T \right]$$

Under this measure all asset price ratios expressed with Z as the denominator are martingales:

$$E_t^Z \left[\frac{X_T}{Z_T} \right] = \frac{B_t}{Z_t} E_t^B[X_T/B_T]$$

$$= \frac{B_t}{Z_t} \frac{X_t}{B_t} = \frac{X_t}{Z_t}$$

For example if we have a European option with a payoff at time T given as C_T we have that the value of the derivative today is simply

$$V_0 = E_0^B \left[\frac{C_T}{B_T} \right]$$

Now with stochastic interest rates B_T is random, so the valuation requires the evaluation of two random quantities expressed as a ratio C_T and B_T. But we can change measure to the T-measure by

$$V_0 = E_0^B \left[\frac{C_T}{B_T} \right]$$

$$= E_0^B[P(T,T)/B_T] E_0^B \left[\left(\frac{P(T,T)/B_T}{E_0^B[P(T,T)/B_T]} \right) C_T \right]$$

$$= P(0,T) E_0^T[C_T]$$

In the above we have normalized both B_0 and $P(T,T)$ to 1.

11.7   Continuous-time term structure models

Over the past twenty years, research by both academics and finance practitioners has evolved from fairly simple models to more complex ones. A number of different approaches have been used. At first models focused on the evolution of the short rate. This formed the basis for Vasicek's model and the Cox, Ingersoll, and Ross model. Since then three other approaches have been used. The HJM approach models the evolution of forward rates. A related approach models the evolution of bond prices directly, and the final approach models the state-price density directly. This approach has strong similarities with the rest of asset pricing. We now give the briefest of introductions to these four approaches.

11.7.1   Short rate models

1. Specify an Ito process for the short rate.
2. Solve model to give implied bond and derivative prices.
3. Adjust parameters so as to best fit the most heavily traded and liquid instruments.
4. Use model to price less-liquid or 'exotic' instrument.

Basic approach

Suppose that the instantaneous short rate r follows an Ito process:

$$dr = m(r)dt + \sigma(r)dW$$

A fundamental result which we shall not prove is that the value today (time 0) of an interest rate security with payoff at time T of F_T is given by

$$E\left[e^{-\bar{r}T}F_T\right]$$

where $\bar{r}$ is the time-average value of r from 0 to T, and the expectation is taken with respect to the risk-neutral process. Define $P(T)$ the price of the T period unit discount bond. Then it follows immediately that

$$P(T) = E\left[e^{-\bar{r}T}\right]$$

Defining the continuously compounded yield on this bond by

$$R(T) = \frac{-\ln P(T)}{T}$$

we have a relation between zero rates and the interest rate process:

$$R(T) = \frac{-\ln E[e^{-\bar{r}T}]}{T}$$

The Vasicek model

In this specification, the short rate r follows a risk-adjusted Ito process of the following form:

$$dr = a(b-r)dt + \sigma\,dW$$

This specification has the interesting feature that the short rate is mean-reverting to a long-run value of b. Note that if r gets well below b then the drift becomes very positive tending to increase the rate, conversely if r becomes very high, then the drift becomes negative tending to pull r back to its long-run level. Vasicek shows that when the short rate is r_0 a discount bond of maturity T is priced by

$$P(r,T) = A(T)e^{-r_0 B(T)}$$

where $A()$ and $B()$ are complicated functions of a, b, and σ, the parameters determining the short rate process. Note they do not depend on r.

The Cox–Ingersoll–Ross (CIR) model

In this specification, the short rate r follows a risk-adjusted Ito process of the following form:

$$dr = a(b-r)dt + \sigma\sqrt{r}\,dW$$

It differs from the Vasicek process in that volatility is proportional to $\sqrt{r}$. This has the effect of guaranteeing that interest rates remain positive. The pricing formula has the same form as in the Vasicek model but the functions $A(T)$ and $B(T)$ are different.

Black–Derman–Toy model

In the continuous time version of this model, the instantaneous short r follows a risk-adjusted process of the form:

$$d\ln r = a(.)dt + \sigma_t\, dW$$

11.7.2   Discount bond modelling

We start by assuming a complete set of zero-coupon bonds with maturities at all dates. Prices at t for a bond paying one dollar at T is denoted $P(t,T)$. Dynamics are specified by

$$\frac{dP(t,T)}{P(t,T)} = \mu(t,T)dt + \Sigma(t,T)\cdot dW_t$$

where W_t is a set of n independent Wiener processes, and $\Sigma(t,T)$ is an n-vector of sensitivities to these shocks. Under the risk-neutral measure all assets (including zero-coupon bonds) have drifts equal to the short rate. Under the risk-neutral measure discount bond price dynamics are

$$\frac{dP(t,T)}{P(t,T)} = r_t\, dt + \Sigma(t,T)\cdot dW_t$$

Recall that for stock prices we have the solution

$$S_t = S_0 \exp\left[\int_{s=0}^{t} \mu_s\, ds\right] \exp\left[\int_{s=0}^{t} \sigma_s\, dW_s - \frac{1}{2}\int_{s=0}^{t} \sigma_s^2\, ds\right]$$

Using the same approach as for stock prices we can write a solution for bond prices as

$$P(t,T) = P(0,T) \exp\left[\int_{s=0}^{t} r_s\, ds\right] \exp\left[\int_{s=0}^{t} \Sigma(s,T)dW_s - \frac{1}{2}\int_{s=0}^{t} \Sigma(s,T)^2\, ds\right]$$

where $\Sigma(s,T)^2$ is shorthand for the dot product $\Sigma(s,T)\cdot\Sigma(s,T)$ which is simply the sum of the squared elements of $\Sigma(s,T)$. Now the money-market account has value at t of $B(t) = \exp\left[\int_{s=0}^{t} r_s\, ds\right]$ so that the formula can be simplified to

$$P(t,T) = P(0,T)B(t)\exp\left[\int_{s=0}^{t} \Sigma(s,T)dW_s - \frac{1}{2}\int_{s=0}^{t}\Sigma(s,T)^2\, ds\right]$$

As this approach does not specify the money-market directly we need to solve for it. This is done by setting $T = t$ to get

$$P(t,t) = P(0,t)B(t)\exp\left[\int_{s=0}^{t}\Sigma(s,t)dW_s - \frac{1}{2}\int_{s=0}^{t}\Sigma(s,t)^2\, ds\right]$$

$$B(t) = P(0,t)^{-1}\exp\left[-\int_{s=0}^{t}\Sigma(s,t)dW_s + \frac{1}{2}\int_{s=0}^{t}\Sigma(s,t)^2\, ds\right]$$

Replacing this expression for the money-market account into the first expression we get

$$P(t,T) = \frac{P(0,T)}{P(0,t)}\frac{\exp\left[\int_{s=0}^{t}\Sigma(s,T)dW_s - \frac{1}{2}\int_{s=0}^{t}\Sigma(s,T)^2\, ds\right]}{\exp\left[\int_{s=0}^{t}\Sigma(s,t)dW_s - \frac{1}{2}\int_{s=0}^{t}\Sigma(s,t)^2\, ds\right]}$$

Denoting the forward price as at zero for a bond deliverable at t with maturity T by $F(0, P(t,T))$ we can write this as

$$P(t,T) = F(0,P(t,T))\frac{\exp\left[\int_{s=0}^{t}\Sigma(s,T)dW_s - \frac{1}{2}\int_{s=0}^{t}\Sigma(s,T)^2\, ds\right]}{\exp\left[\int_{s=0}^{t}\Sigma(s,t)dW_s - \frac{1}{2}\int_{s=0}^{t}\Sigma(s,t)^2\, ds\right]}$$

This is a forward price formula in which bond prices are determined solely by the initial term structure and by the volatility function $\Sigma(.,.)$.

11.7.3   State price density approach

A well-known result from asset pricing is that the price of any asset at t with a payoff C_t at T can be given as

$$V_t = E_t\left[C_T m_T\right]/m_t$$

where m_t is a random variable called the *pricing kernel*, or *state price density* or *stochastic discount factor*. It follows that the price of any zero-coupon bond is simply

$$B(t, T) = \frac{E_t[m_T]}{m_t}$$

Modelling proceeds by constructing various processes for m_t. Rogers (1997) and Campbell, Lo, and Mackinlay (1997) develop a variety of models using this approach.

11.8   References

11.8.1   General

1. Shimko, D.C. *Finance in Continuous Time: A Primer*, Kolb Publishing Company.
2. Merton, R.C.   *Continuous-Time   Finance*,   Chapter 3,   Blackwell Publishers.
3. Baxter, M. and A. Rennie *Financial Calculus: An Introduction to Derivative Pricing*, Cambridge University Press.
4. Neftci, S.H. *An Introduction to the Mathematics of Financial Derivatives*, Academic Press, London.
5. Duffie, D. *Dynamic Asset Pricing Theory*, Princeton University Press.

11.8.2   Term structure models

1. *Vasicek and Beyond* Ed. Lane Hughston, Risk Publications
2. Campbell, Lo, and Mackinlay *The Econometrics of Financial Markets*, Princeton University Press, NJ.
3. Rogers, L.C.G. (1997) 'One for All,' *RISK*, 10(3).

Index

Printed and bound by CPI Group (UK) Ltd, Croydon, CR0 4YY

08/05/2025

01864776-0002

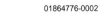